OVER 60 EASY TO UNDERSTAND DIAGRAMS

CRYPTO NEW RICH

From Bitcoin Beginner to Financial Freedom in 5 Years

TROY HARRIS

CONTENTS

FREE RESOURCES

DOWNLOAD THE FREE RESOURCES

Includes ✓ All the Diagrams from the Book

See CryptoNewRich.com/resources

** We give you full permission to use these visual diagrams in your social posts & communication materials provided they have our branding watermarks as per these free resources.*

GET THE VIDEO TRAINING

We have found from experience that people learn in a variety of different ways. If you find that you learn well from video, visuals, and audio then you may get excellent value from the video training that accompanies this book in a 1 + 1 = 3 type of way.

There is a famous old story of the man who is cutting down a tree and it is taking a long time because he won't stop and take the time to sharpen the saw.

The reality is as investors we spend a lot of money on our portfolios. But your greatest investment is in your knowledge, mindset, emotional and financial intelligence as you bring yourself to every investment and every deal.

Take the time to stop and sharpen your saw with this cost-effective video training. You'll get your desired results faster, while also reducing your risks of making costly mistakes.

**The above-listed investment in your education is risk-free, as we offer a 100% money-back guarantee. In the unlikely event that you have watched the training and did not get amazing value from it, just reach out to our team, and we will refund your money in full.*

INTRODUCTION

The Greatest Wealth Creation Opportunity of a Lifetime

"Crypto is the biggest opportunity. It dwarfs everything else in terms of risk adjusted returns." – Raoul Pal, co-founder and CEO of Real Vision

I started my career in customer service, but always had a keen eye on the tech space. I could see the creation of the Internet was the biggest opportunity to date. When I discovered crypto, everything changed for me as I saw there was a new *'fastest horse'* when it came to wealth creation.

In 2017, I had a 'lightbulb switching on' moment. I really understood Bitcoin and could see with great certainty that this was going to keep appreciating faster than anything we had ever seen before.

Many laughed at me and every time there was a dip, they would ask me, 'How is your Magical Internet Money going now?'

Despite the naysayers, I kept consistently investing into the space. Time has proven my gut feel from all those years ago to be true and accurate. Now, no one seems to be laughing at me and asking me about my crazy internet money, other than 'Would you mind teaching me?'

Crypto is the best investment opportunity that has ever been given to retail investors like you and I. This is also the first time in history where retail investors got to front run (get into a market) and obtain better buy prices than institutional investors.

It's the best performing asset class of all time, the fastest adoption of any technology in all time outside of AI, and the fastest generation of wealth in the shortest period of time. Why anyone would not be involved in this market is crazy to me.

The prize of getting this right is freedom and your dream life by design.

Crypto and Investing But Much More

"Formal education will make you a living; self-education will make you a fortune." – Jim Rohn, American entrepreneur, author and motivational speaker

First, a little bit about *Crypto New Rich – From Bitcoin Beginner to Financial Freedom in Five Years*. It's about crypto and it's about investing, but it's actually about a whole bunch more than that.

I think I've read every single crypto book on Amazon, and they all have one thing in common – they are about the technical nature of cryptocurrencies.

I'm a realist. I know that 99.99% of people like yourself don't get into crypto to learn about cryptography, hash rates and block sizes. I believe you are in crypto to make yourself wealthy so that you can live life on your terms, not someone else's.

That's why this book isn't highly technical in nature. Instead, it's focussed on what you need to learn and who you need to become to be part of the Crypto New Rich. I'm in a good position to share that with you as I've done it myself and helped many others to achieve it.

By achieving a very high level of skills in investing and business, I've been able to use that to create a multi-million dollar portfolio, multiple income streams, an amazing lifestyle design and freedom for my family. I will show you the roadmap so you can engineer similar results in your life.

How Money Flows With Investing

In crypto, money flows to those who know how to get in and out of the markets at the right times, how to consistently adapt to market cycles, and how to string together multiple market cycles to multiply their capital.

HOW MONEY FLOWS WITH INVESTING

Money Naturally Flows From Those Who Don't Know What They Are Doing to Those Who Do

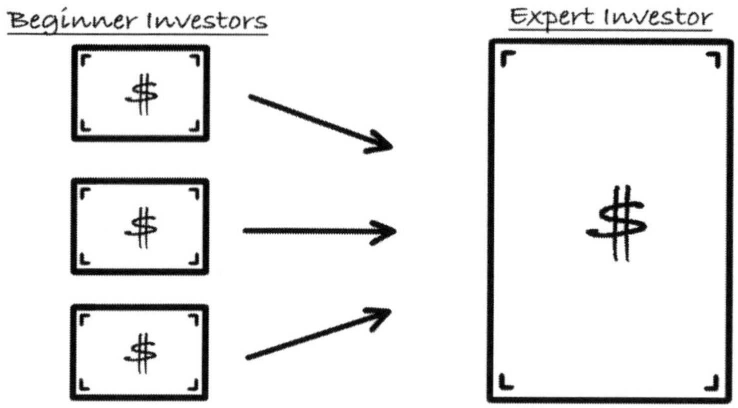

*The Expert Investor understands the Markets Cycles & Times Entry & Exits to Maximize Profits. The Beginner Investor Does Not Exit the Market at the Ideal Timing & Loses Their Money

Specialize and Become Smart Money

When I was younger, well-meaning people advised me that I needed to diversify into lots of different asset classes. While they meant well, I noticed that none of these people were wealthy.

As I got a little older and wiser, I noticed that the people who became very wealthy specialized in one area that they learned well and created themselves an advantage in. They then built wealth in this one area and parked their winnings in other asset classes, like property, over time to preserve their wealth.

What You Want & What You Need

Becoming wealthy and engineering success isn't about luck – it's about transforming and changing to become the type of person who makes money and succeeds in any environment.

You could drop me off in just about any country (maybe exclude war zones as I'm a peaceful kind of guy) in any market or industry, and I could make money. I have learned what it takes and evolved to have that mindset and skillset.

You want to become part of the Crypto New Rich. The good thing is that it's a learnable skill. I have this saying: "*You bring yourself to the deal,*" so you need to show up with the very best version of yourself. That is why this book and training is designed with this two-part holistic approach.

THE TWO PARTS OF THE

CRYPTO NEW RICH BOOK

1.	2.
What You Need to Know About Crypto to Join the New Rich	Who You Need to Become to be at the Right Level to Join the Crypto New Rich

The more time we spend together, the more you will learn that very little that I do is a coincidence; it's all engineered and by design.

This book is short in length on purpose (so it feels consumable). It has logical diagram models to tell visual stories right throughout it (as a picture tells a thousand words).

It is designed to be read in order as one thing builds on the next, but if you prefer, feel free to jump straight to the sections that interest you most.

The Rat Race – What if the Masses Have it Wrong?

All my life, I was taught to go to school and *'work hard'* to *'get a good job'* and *'work hard'* to hopefully be able to *'save enough money'* to *'retire'* as an old man with enough wealth to survive.

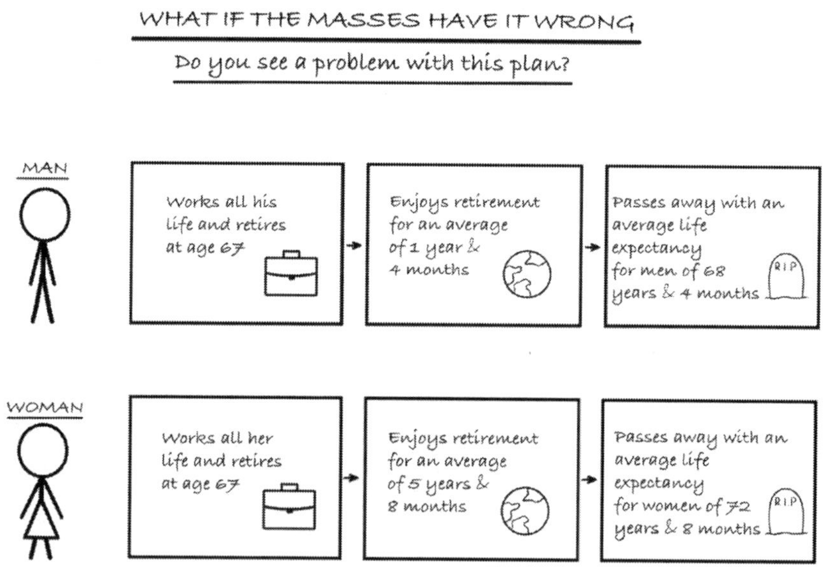

If the average retirement age is roughly 67 years old, and according to Wikipedia, the average life expectancy is 68 years and 4 months for males and 72 years and 8 months for women – this doesn't leave much time for *'living'* at the end of a hard-working life.

I acknowledge that these are global averages, and some affluent countries will have longer lifespans than the average, but still, it's pretty ordinary.

This seems to me like an outdated flawed plan, and while it is how I started, it is certainly not how I lived my life once I found an alternative route, as outlined in this book.

What is amazing is when you look at that diagram above, you don't need to be a rocket scientist to figure out that it's not a very smart plan. However, it's the recipe that most people, even highly educated people, will live by.

Every time I have to go on a train going into the city for business, I hear people complaining, saying things like *"My job sucks"* and *"I Can't wait until it's Friday."*

But most people never really do anything about it. They believe it's acceptable to do something they have been unhappy with for years without ever seeking or taking action on an alternative solution.

To me, it's like a fairy tale in which the wicked witch has put a *'fog'* over the land, and 97% of people are just happy to go through the motions.

You Can Have It All

The reality is we live in a very special time in world history that is relatively peaceful, and it's a world of abundance for those who are willing to learn what it takes, become who it takes, take action to make it happen, and follow through until you achieve it. You really can have it all:

- The Investments
- The Money
- The Lifestyle

- The Freedom
- The Knowledge
- The Mindset
- The Emotional Intelligence
- The Family and Friends
- The Love
- The Travel
- The Nice House
- The Toys
- The Choices
- The Great Health and Fitness
- The Safe Certain Future
- The Ability to Give Back and Make a Positive Impact

If you get it right, the prize is joining the new rich and living in the top 1%.

I'm guessing you really want it all, or you wouldn't be reading this book. I've achieved these things (consistently working on health and fitness, which is the most important thing) and also helped so many others.

Not a Financial Advisor

Boring but important: The lessons in this book are for educational purposes only. The author, Troy Harris, is not a registered financial advisor in any state or territory.

Registered financial advisors have a never-ending list of constraints on what they are and are not allowed to do or recommend for their clients. Most financial advisors are excited about 8–12% returns per year (not per day, week or month like crypto in a bull run).

Troy Harris is a crypto multi-millionaire whose goal is to share with other many of the lessons from the journey that helped him become financially and time free. Like with all investing please do your own research and never invest more than you are comfortable to lose.

Chapter 1 – Five Steps to the Crypto New Rich

The Essential Ingredients for a Cake to Rise

If you don't add all the right ingredients, a cake won't rise. A cake needs a leavening agent like baking powder, baking soda or self-raising flour. If you leave out this one element, you can go to all the effort, but you won't get what is considered a successful-looking cake.

Over my 8+ years in crypto, I learned that five ingredients are essential for a crypto, portfolio to rise and stay high in the long term. Let's explore these briefly now and then we will go deeper in the chapters that follow.

Five Steps to Crypto New Rich for the Prize of Freedom and Your Dream Life By Design

"At some stage in your career you will get to the point where the money comes at you harder and faster than you ever thought possible, and you will wonder where it has been hiding this whole time." – Greg Cassar.

My good friend Greg said that to me when we first met years ago, and it blew me away. I have experienced that at brief times in my entrepreneurial career, but nothing of the magnitude of how fast the money comes at you when you get it right with crypto.

It's exciting times indeed. We have been born into a very lucky time in human history as investors, as the markets are global and still young enough that even the small investor can still find his/her place and thrive.

After lots of trial and error and figuring things out the hard way, I have concluded that there are five essential steps on the road to the Crypto New Rich. If you don't know, understand, or do these five things, then effectively your investment 'cake won't rise'.

THE CRYPTO PENTAGON

The Essential 5 Steps on the Road to the Crypto New Rich

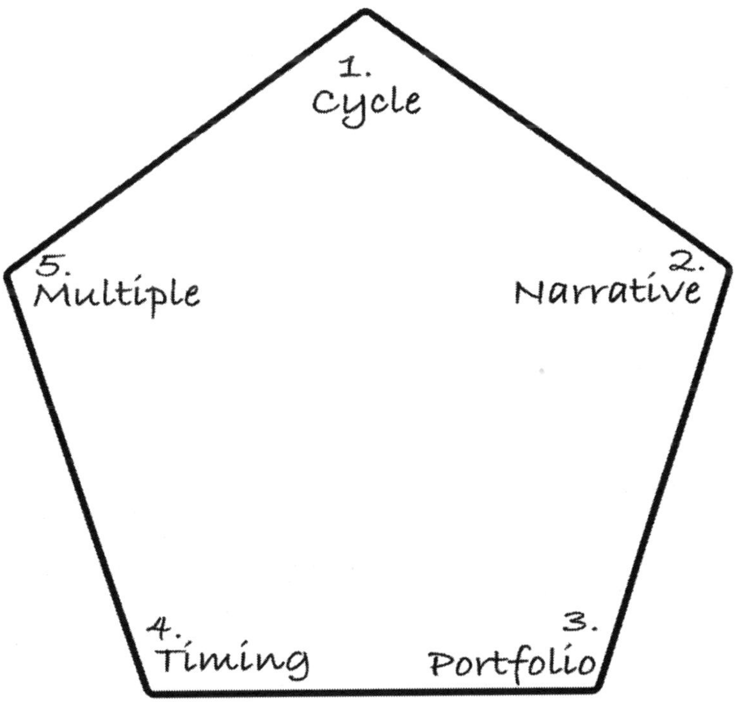

We will unpack these in detail in the coming chapters, but effectively, they are:

1. **Cycle:** Understand the four-year cycle; historically, this has been the key to your success.
2. **Narrative:** Learn, pay attention to and invest in the stories/themes/narratives that the market is excited about.
3. **Portfolio:** Build a diversified, high-growth portfolio that ties in with the winning narratives.
4. **Timing:** Based on your knowledge of the four-year cycle and history, the time when to get in and out of the market and how to maximize your chances of getting it right.
5. **Multiple:** How to combine multiple cycles and compound your capital to create long-term generational wealth.

PART 1 – WHAT YOU NEED TO KNOW ABOUT CRYPTO TO JOIN THE NEW RICH

Chapter 2 – Blockchain and Crypto Essentials

"Cryptocurrency will be the biggest opportunity for wealth creation in our lifetime." – Anthony Pompliano, international entrepreneur and technology investor

Quick Overview

If you are already experienced in crypto, you may choose to skip this chapter. The goal is to provide some easy-to-understand definitions of key terms required to understand this fast-developing industry and its associated exponential investment opportunities.

At the end of the chapter, we will look at common objections people have and some informed investor responses to those objections.

What is a Blockchain?

The Oxford dictionary defines a Blockchain as *'a system in which a record of transactions, especially those made in a cryptocurrency, is maintained across computers that are linked in a peer-to-peer network.'*

A blockchain is a distributed digital ledger. Okay, so what's a ledger? Think back to an old merchant sailing ship in pirate-type days. The ship's captain pulls into the port, and he sells a whole bunch of bananas and might be taking on board some apples to sell. In his ship's ledger, the captain writes down how many bananas they sold and for what price. He also records the number of apples they purchased and the price in the ledger.

That's what the ledger used to be, but what's the problem? If you lose that ledger, you lose the record of what's happened.

Once we entered the digital age, everything moved into centralized databases. The problem is that a couple of big companies have these big databases, and they own all the data, so you have to trust them.

Blockchain, and really Bitcoin, which was the first blockchain technology of this type, is a distributed ledger. Multiple different validating nodes on the network verify every transaction that happens so that no one can ever cheat it.

Adding a Trust Layer to the Internet

With the traditional Internet, if I had a file, I could give you a copy of that file. Now, there are two files, but which one is the original file and which one isn't? You can see why this wouldn't work for digital money.

Blockchain effectively has added a trust layer to the Internet because it's a unique entry on a ledger that has been validated and verified to be unique and true at the time it was written to the Blockchain. It is cryptographically written into the ledger, therefore it is immutable and can never replicated.

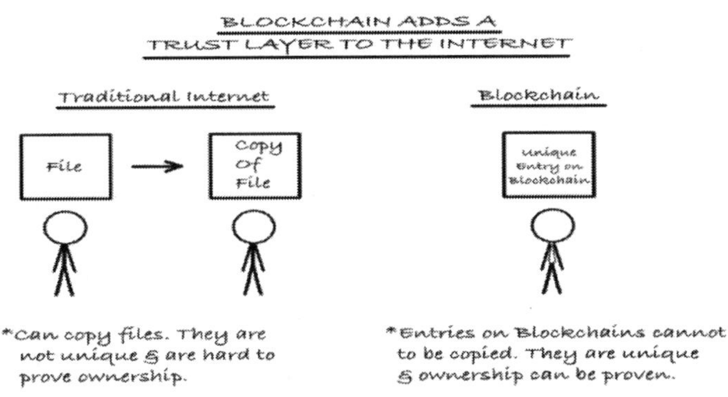

Cryptocurrency

A cryptocurrency is a digital or virtual currency secured by cryptography. As it is built on blockchain technology, it is impossible to counterfeit or double-spend. Bitcoin was the world's first, and at the time of this writing, most valuable cryptocurrency. It was launched in January 2009.

Altcoins

Altcoins are alternative cryptocurrencies that were launched after Bitcoin. The term 'Altcoins' means alternative coins to Bitcoin. Examples of Altcoins include Ethereum, Solana and Polygon.

Coins & Tokens

These two terms get interchanged a bit, and it can be confusing. A simple way of looking at it is this…

Coins are created on and operate on blockchains – they function primarily as digital currency.

Tokens are created on and operate on blockchains and are typically used to create and manage assets, access services, or represent ownership of physical assets on these blockchains.

Moving forward, the evolution of the technology is pointing towards the future where everything of value in the world will eventually be a token on a blockchain. This includes things like stocks, bonds, commodities, collectible cars, and real estate. It's literally a line item on a public ledger, and every transaction of value will happen in digital assets.

Stablecoins

Stablecoins are a type of cryptocurrency whose value is tied to another asset class to keep a stable, steady value. The most popular kind of Stablecoins is fiat-backed Stablecoins, which are tied to currencies such as the US dollar.

As of this writing the most popular Stablecoin in the world is Tether (USDT). Buying Tether is effectively like buying US dollars. You can buy it on one exchange, and then easily transfer it to another exchange in seconds, and then use it to buy cryptocurrencies or other digital assets.

What is an Exchange?

A cryptocurrency exchange is a website and app platform that functions similarly to an online brokerage platform. It provides you with the tools to transfer your native currency into and out of and then gives you the tools you need to be able to buy and sell cryptocurrencies like Bitcoin and most common Altcoins at agreed market rates. The exchange will take a small commission to do the transaction for you.

Bull Markets & Bear Markets

While not unique to crypto alone, the terms bull market and bear market are key concepts to understand as we build into the four-year cycle concept.

A bull market refers to a financial market condition in which prices are rising or are expected to rise. The optimism, investor confidence, and expectations of strong results that typically accompany bull markets can drive further increases in asset prices.

A bear market is characterized by falling prices and typically shrouded in pessimism. During bear markets, investors often seek to offload their holdings to minimize losses, thereby perpetuating the downward price trend.

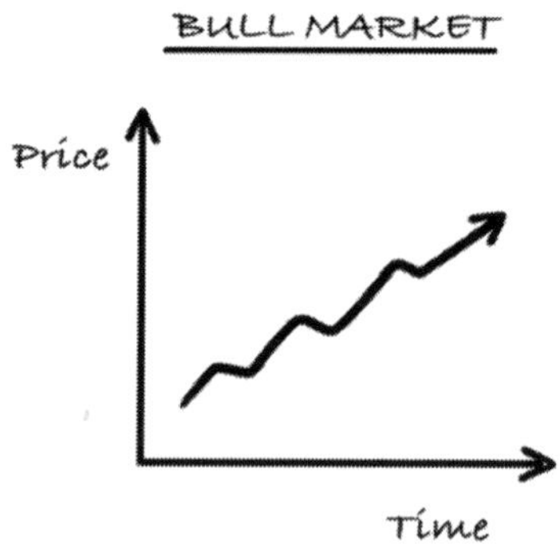

Dollar Cost Averaging

It's very hard to pick the exact bottom of a market cycle to enter a buying position, or the exact top of a market cycle to exit a position.

The term 'dollar cost averaging' refers to spreading your investments over multiple time periods, such as weeks or months, to average out your buy or sell position. The goal is to use dollar cost averaging to buy the bottom or sell the top of a market cycle.

This approach gives you a far greater chance of achieving your investing goals than if you were to do all your buying or exiting of the market at one point of time.

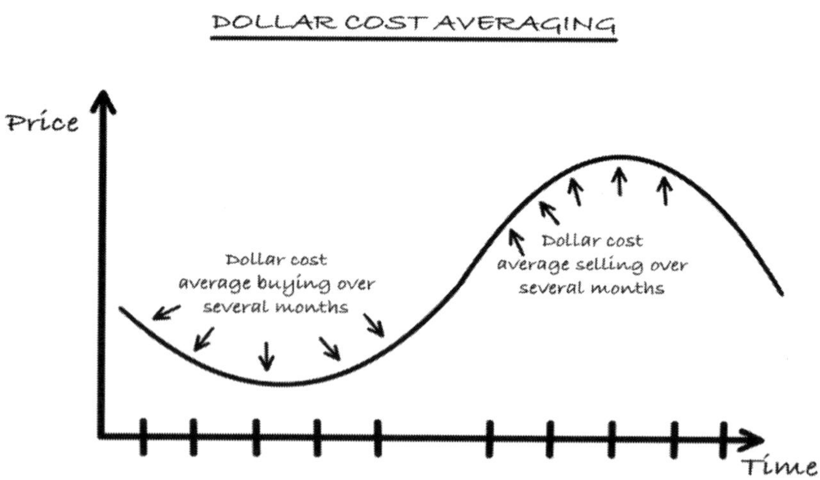

Overcoming Common Objections

"Don't let your own personal opinions and biases get in the way between you and getting wealthy." – Mal Emery, Australian entrepreneur and marketing expert

Every month, I meet people who say, *"Crypto is a scam"* or *"What if the Government shuts it down*?" I think it's a real shame because they are letting their own fear and noise within themselves slow them down from participating in the greatest wealth-creation opportunity of our lifetimes.

People with these common objections haven't 'done the work' yet, meaning they have not invested the hours to learn it.

American entrepreneur, executive chairman and co-founder of Microstrategy, Michael Saylor has an incredible saying of *"Everybody gets Bitcoin at the price they deserve."* This means that once people are open to it and have learned about it, they will get into it, but the longer they wait, the more the price appreciates.

Here are some common crypto objections and logical responses to help those on the fence trying to decide if they want to be involved in the next evolution of the Internet and money.

OVERCOMING COMMON OBJECTIONS

Objection	Informed Investor Response
Bitcoin is bad for the environment	The majority of the Bitcoin miners have now moved to renewable energy.
It's too volatile	This is true, but it is the case in all young & rapidly growing markets.
What if the Government shuts it down	Regulation of the industry is in it's early stages, but no Government can shut it down as it is a global trust & value layer to the Internet.
It's used by criminals	This certainly was the case early on. Due to it's public ledger nature most transaction are traceable & not ideal for crime.
Bitcoin doesn't have any real value	Bitcoin value is determined by supply & demand as it has limited supply & a large demand to own it.

Chapter 3 – Bitcoin Essentials

"I think of Bitcoin the same way I think about the early Internet. They didn't see it coming and now it's a viable form of currency... I think the government is freaking out." – Joe Rogan, host of the world-popular *Joe Rogan Experience* podcast

You Can't 'Unsee Bitcoin' Once You Understand It

I'd heard of the word Bitcoin in passing in the 2010s but didn't give it a second thought as I didn't know anything about it. The only person who had suggested buying some to me was a friend who was using it for online poker then! Therefore, as you can imagine, it didn't really click in my head as a viable investment opportunity.

I'm lucky that I've always been able to see and understand new technologies before most. Therefore, when my friend mentioned again in 2016 that he was no longer using Bitcoin for online poker and was just buying and holding it because its price kept increasing, I knew I had to at least take a look.

There wasn't as much good information available then as there is now, but I went deep down the rabbit hole of research. I remember lying awake at night with my head spinning with how exciting it was, but it still puzzled me that most people were blind to it and what was happening.

With the full support of my amazing wife Nicky, we decided to go all in and essentially, in my wife's words, "Live like Uni students for four years." Every last dollar I could get my hand on after paying living expenses went into this space. We sold our house and went all in. Never had I been more convinced of a technology before.

As Michael Saylor says, *"Allocate 100 hours of your life to study Bitcoin. The average person is going to work 80,000 hours to make money; you should work 100 hours of your life to keep it."* I most certainly spent thousands more hours studying it than that. It turned out to be a bit of a masterstroke that will create generational wealth for my family in the years to come, as Bitcoin goes into the millions and tens of millions per coin is my belief.

What is Bitcoin?

"Bitcoin is one of the most important discoveries of humanity... perfect digital scarcity, and I'm not aware of any better store of value. We desperately need it to separate money from state." – DC Roth, Bitcoin investor and YouTuber

Bitcoin is a revolutionary change because it is the world's first digital money, but it is much more than that.

The Bitcoin network uses Blockchain technology to be a decentralized international payments network that doesn't rely on banks or governments.

Bitcoin is not a company or organization. It is a standard or protocol. It's built on a set of mathematical rules that everyone who participates in the Bitcoin network agrees on.

Bitcoin lets us send and receive value to anyone, anywhere, anytime, without needing a middleman.

Bitcoin is the only crypto currency that has secured its place in the world in the long term.

It can get a bit technical describing it. All you really need to know is *"Bitcoin is like digital gold. It's the world's first Internet money, and you can store or transfer value with it."*

Bitcoin as Digital Gold

"Unpopular but true: Bitcoin is the most significant monetary advance since the creation of coinage." – Edward Snowden

Bitcoin is a store of value often described as 'digital gold.' The 21 million Bitcoin limited supply is hardcoded into Bitcoin's protocol. The purpose of the limited supply is to mimic the scarcity and durable value of precious metals like gold.

This also allows Bitcoin to act as a hedge against inflation. At the time of writing, Bitcoin's market cap is only a small percentage of the market cap of gold. However, I expect Bitcoin to flip gold in market cap in the years to come because of the reasons outlined below.

BITCOIN AS DIGITAL GOLD

Feature	Ⓑ	(gold bar)
Store Of Value	✓	✓
Divisibility	High	Low
Portability	High	Medium
Supply Capped	✓	X
Easily Transactable	High	Low
Stable Price	Low	High
Growth In Value	Fast	Slow
Decentralized	High	Low

Bitcoin's Limited Supply

Bitcoin is designed with a fixed supply limit of 21 million coins. This unique feature differentiates it from traditional fiat currencies around the world, which can be printed without limit by governments and central banks.

The controlled supply of Bitcoin is managed through a process known as mining, where new Bitcoins are created as a reward for miners who process transactions and secure the network.

The limited supply of Bitcoin has significant implications for its valuation and economic impact. It has contributed to the rise of cryptocurrency prices, as investors bet on its increasing scarcity over time, driving up demand.

Additionally, it has influenced Bitcoin's adoption as a store of value, with many investors viewing it as an asset class like precious metals. Its supply schedule is written in code, which is predictable and transparent.

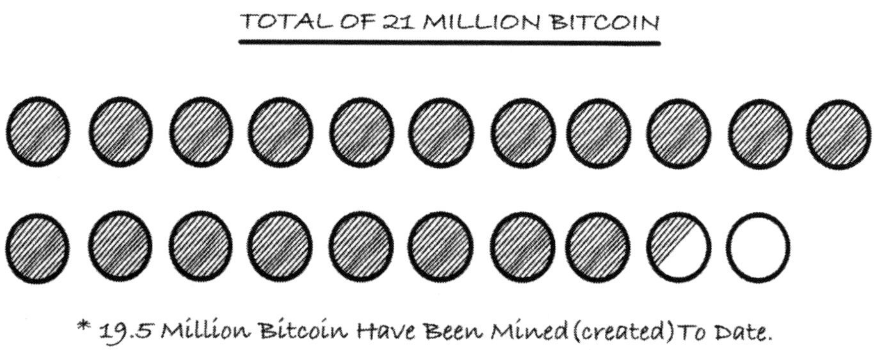

Many estimates suggest that as much as 30% of Bitcoin's total supply, or as many as six million Bitcoin, have been lost or can no longer be accessed by their owners. This would put the real number of available Bitcoin well below the 21 million number, making it even more scarce.

Unit of Account or Global Reserve Currency of the World?

The US Dollar is currently the reserve currency of the world. It may stay this way for many years to come, although the US government is devaluing its currency rapidly due to the continual printing of dollars.

Because of its fixed, limited supply and its global nature spanning all borders, Bitcoin may become the measure of value that other financial systems are compared to moving forward. This would be like how many currencies were pegged to gold as a standard of value in previous generations.

The Money of the People

"Bitcoin is the beginning of something great: a currency without a government, something necessary and imperative." – Nassim Taleb, Lebanese-American essayist and mathematical statistician

The out-of-control money printing of the US Dollar has led to the devaluing of once strong and stable first-world currencies. The consistent decline of their store of value is now creeping in more and more and affecting everyday life all over the world, regardless of your country's stature.

Unfortunately, in even less prosperous nations around the world, the people are losing even more purchasing power of their native currencies because of decisions made by their governments that are completely beyond their control. In many nations, Bitcoin offers a glimmer of hope for preserving their wealth as it is truly global, beyond any government's control, and appreciates in value rather than depreciating.

Purchasing Power

"Bitcoin is a new hope for the world... Bitcoin restores economic independence to entrepreneurs by giving them a way to store wealth

that cannot be plundered. Working-class people now have a savings medium that does not force them to take unnecessary risks or extend their working lives in a race to outpace inflation." – Robert Breedlove, American entrepreneur, writer, philosopher and Bitcoin investor

When governments print more money, it leads to inflation, which results in less purchasing power for the people. In the example below, you can see that for $200, you no longer get as many groceries as you did in the past.

Bitcoin is working the exact opposite. Because of its fixed supply, it does not have any inflation. Its growing demand causes the price of Bitcoin to continually increase over time.

In the example below, the purchasing power of one Bitcoin is getting stronger, and it takes less Bitcoin over time to be able to buy a house. Moving forward, it is my opinion that only a fraction of a Bitcoin will be enough value to buy a house.

BITCOINS FIXED SUPPLY &

EFFECT ON PURCHASING POWER

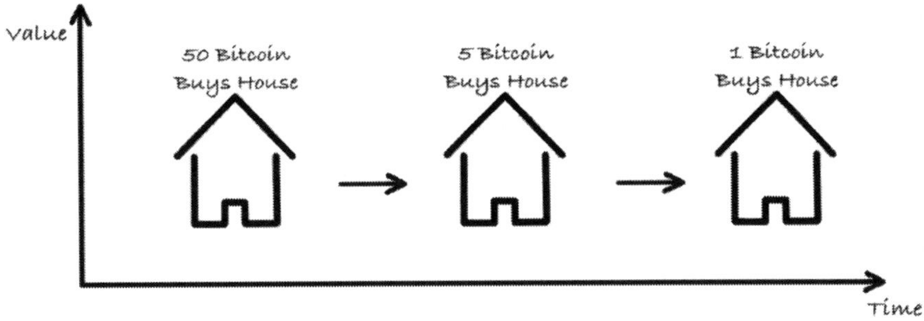

Satoshi & Bitcoin's Origin

Satoshi Nakamoto is the pseudonym of the mysterious individual or group that developed Bitcoin. Bitcoin was first introduced in a 2008 paper titled *Bitcoin: A Peer-to-Peer Electronic Cash System.*

The identity of Satoshi Nakamoto has remained a mystery, with numerous speculations but no conclusive evidence pointing to any person or group. Satoshi was actively involved in developing and modifying the Bitcoin software until December 2010. After this, Satoshi's direct involvement with Bitcoin ceased, and his communication with the Bitcoin community dwindled, leaving behind only the written works and emails.

The Bitcoin system came into existence with the mining of the genesis block on 3 January 2009.

Satoshis (SATS)

Moving forward, the value of Bitcoin is going to be far too high for the average investor to buy a whole one. I believe that within five to 10 years, most people will be concerned with SATS rather than Bitcoins as they will be more achievable to own.

Satoshis (SATS) refers to the smallest unit of the Bitcoin cryptocurrency, named after Bitcoin's creator, Satoshi Nakamoto. One Satoshi equals one hundred millionth of a Bitcoin, making it the basic unit in Bitcoin's denomination system.

This allows for fine-grained transactions and reflects Bitcoin's high divisibility, facilitating micro-transactions when the value of a single Bitcoin becomes very high.

SATOSHI'S TO BITCOIN

1 Satoshi	=	0.00000001 BTC
10 Satoshi	=	0.00000010 BTC
100 Satoshi	=	0.00000100 BTC
1,000 Satoshi	=	0.00001000 BTC
10,000 Satoshi	=	0.00010000 BTC
100,000 Satoshi	=	0.00100000 BTC
1,000,000 Satoshi	=	0.01000000 BTC
10,000,000 Satoshi	=	0.10000000 BTC
100,000,000 Satoshi	=	1.00000000 BTC

Bitcoin ETFs

ETF stands for Exchange-Traded Fund. A spot Bitcoin ETF is an exchange-traded fund that tracks the current price of Bitcoin. By holding an equivalent amount of Bitcoin to back every share of the ETF that is sold, the fund is backed by Bitcoin itself.

With the approval of 11 US spot Bitcoin ETFs in January 2024, traditional investors have an even easier way to invest in Bitcoin.

A spot Bitcoin ETF allows investors to gain exposure to the current price of Bitcoin without having to hold the asset itself. This opens up Bitcoin demand to a whole new series of institutional and sovereign (country and state) investors that would not have purchased it previously.

I expect that most countries around the world will create their own Bitcoin Spot ETFs following the US Spot Bitcoin ETF launches, which were the most successful ETF launches of all time.

Where the World is Headed

Ever since the end of the Second World War, the financial world has been based on a notion of *'he or she who owns the most dollars wins.'*

Because of the excessive printing of dollars versus the scarce fixed supply of Bitcoin, I believe we are heading towards a world where *'he or she who owns the most Bitcoin wins.'* We may be there already, but most people don't know or understand it yet.

CHAPTER 4 – MASTERING THE 4 YEAR CYCLE

There is no risk to you with the above-listed investment in your education, as we offer a 100% money-back guarantee. In the unlikely event that you have watched the training and did not get amazing value from it, just reach out to our team, and we will refund your money in full.

First Component in The Crypto Pentagon Framework

'Cycle' – Mastering the four-year cycles is the first component in the Crypto Pentagon Framework.

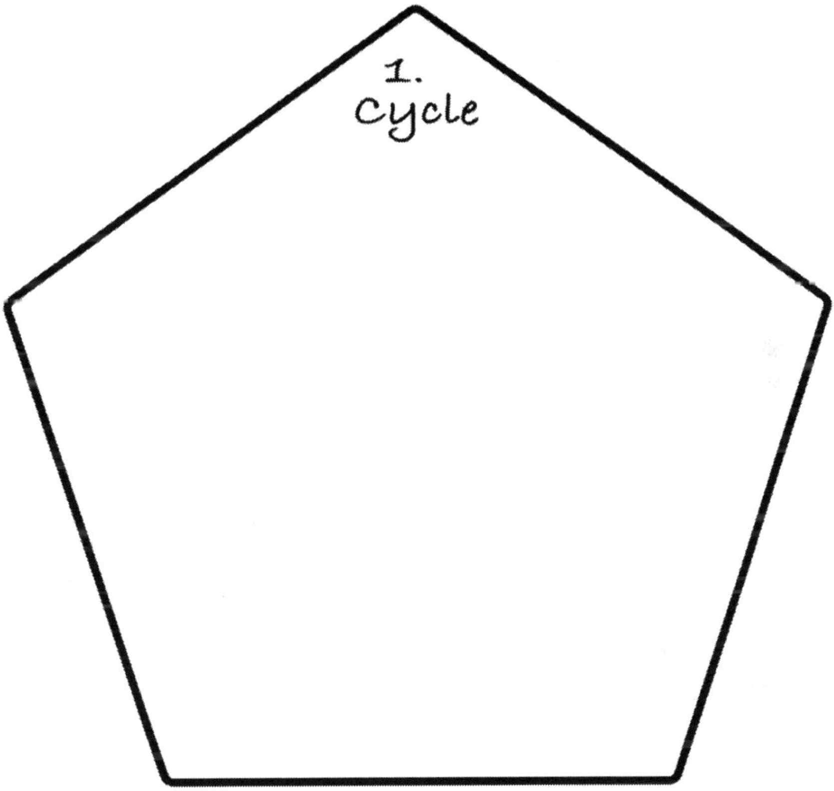

A Very Big Deal

"Data doesn't lie; it tells you exactly what works and what doesn't." – Alex Becker, Tech Entrepreneur

Understanding the Bitcoin four-year cycle is a very big deal. I would say it is the key to moving from an amateur to a more sophisticated investor with a significantly greater chance of success.

I have found myself describing it to people who ask me about it: *"Study and learn the four-year Bitcoin cycle; that is the key to winning in crypto."*

When the first two Bitcoin four-year cycles happened and looked very similar on the graph, I thought, "That is interesting. I wonder if it's a trend." The problem with only two data points is that it can be just a coincidence, so I couldn't make informed decisions based on them. As a result, I didn't know clearly when to get into the market and when to get out of the market with great confidence.

I don't think I'm the only crypto investor who has ridden the bull market all the way up, just to ride the bear market all the way down. I had the foresight not to sell when my positions were down, so I didn't realize any losses. But I did eat some humble pie and had a long, painful three to four-year wait to get back into profits.

Once the same cycle had repeated more than twice, I could see there was a trend, not just a coincidence. We will unpack that for you soon so that you can benefit from these learnings and this largely predictable market cycle, as it currently stands.

The Bitcoin Halving

"We have elected to put our money and faith in a mathematical framework that is free of politics and human error." – Tyler Winklevoss, American Bitcoin investor and founder of Gemini Cryptocurrency Exchange

The controlled supply of Bitcoin is managed through a process known as mining, where new Bitcoins are created as a reward for miners who process transactions and secure the network.

This reward is halved approximately every four years in an event known as "halving." These halving events reduce the rate at which new Bitcoins are created.

The last Bitcoin is expected to be mined around the year 2140. After this point, miners will be compensated purely through transaction fees.

We will explore halving and its impact further in the following sections.

New Bitcoins Mined Per Day

Before the 2024 halving, Bitcoin miners produced around 900 Bitcoin per day. Following the 2024 halving, the miners are now producing around 450 Bitcoin per day. This volume of Bitcoins mined daily will halve roughly every four years until 2140.

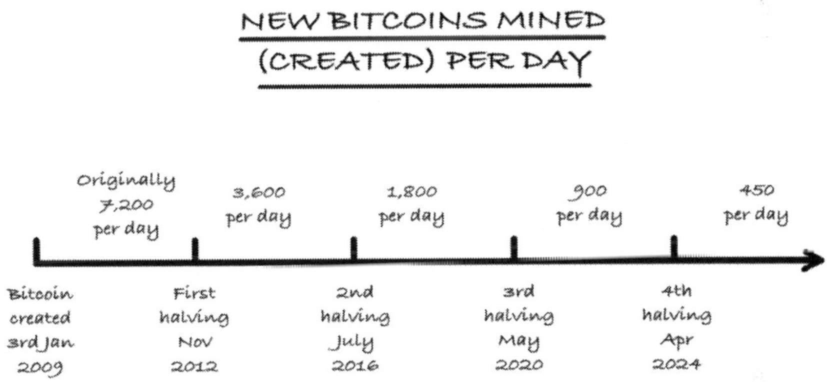

Supply Shock

Imagine there is a gas (petrol) shortage. People still want gas. What will happen to the price of it? It will go up because of supply and demand – School Economics class finally became useful :)

It is believed that the halving events caused the Bitcoin price to increase because of the reduced supply coming onto the market. As basic economics dictates, if you reduce supply while demand stays the same or increases, then prices should rise naturally.

There is some historical evidence for this, as there has consistently been rapid price appreciation and a bull market in the year or two following the Bitcoin halving events.

Often, the actual Bitcoin halving event will have little to no immediate effect on the Bitcoin price but then will come into effect over a short period of time after that. This is the equivalent of a very large seller coming onto the market and buying half of the old available supply of new Bitcoin from the market.

Demand Shock

As Bitcoin continues to appreciate in price, there will be increasing demand from people wanting to participate in that price action.

As Governments around the world print more money, concerned citizens will seek out Bitcoin to store wealth, avoid inflation of their currencies, and lose their real purchasing power.

The biggest demand shock in recent times has been the Bitcoin ETFs. These have opened up Bitcoin as a viable, easy-to-access asset class to large financial institutions, corporations and nation-states. There will continue to be more and more Bitcoin ETFs approved around the world now, continually increasing the demand for Bitcoin.

The Bitcoin Halving's Effect on Price

The diagram below shows that with each halving, the miners produce fewer Bitcoins. At the same time, demand is increasing. This reduced supply and increased demand cause the price of the asset to increase steadily over time.

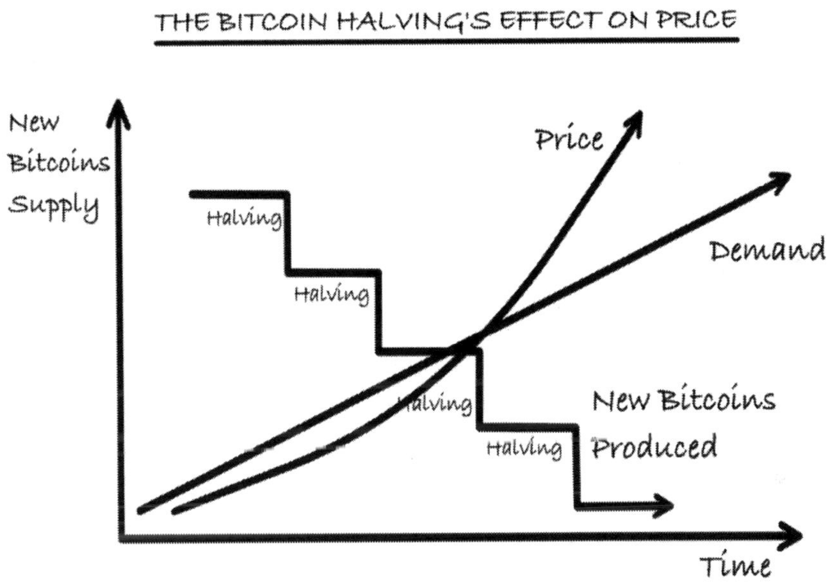

Where Supply & Demand Shock Is Headed = B-Day

I would argue that most people are blind to what is about to happen. A good chess player can think multiple moves ahead. If we think multiple moves ahead to even a few years out, the supply and demand side of Bitcoin is a very wild ride.

Demand will most likely continue to rise exponentially at a rate we have never seen before. This is due to increased volumes from existing ETFs, more international Bitcoin ETFs coming onto the market, more institutional buyers starting to buy, and more nation-states starting to acquire Bitcoin at scale. That doesn't even include demand from retail investors like you and I who want to own more because the price keeps going up.

BITCOIN SUPPLY SHOCK, DEMAND SHOCK & B-DAY

B-Day is When All Available Supply on Exchanges is Gone & Bitcoin Price Appreciates Rapidly & Exponentially

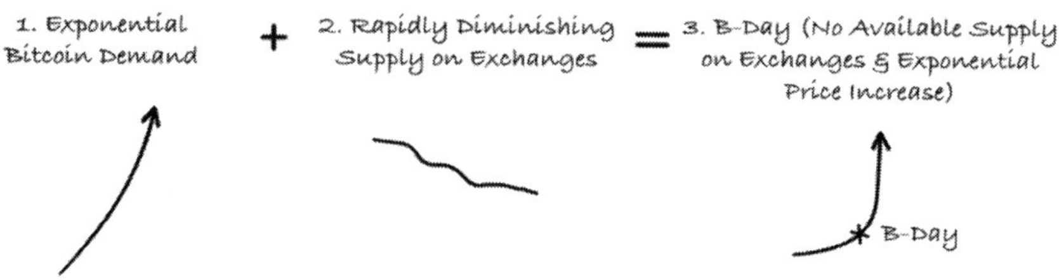

Increasing demand is resulting in the purchasing of Bitcoin being many times greater than the new Bitcoin being mined or made available on the market on a day-by-day basis.

This leaves us in a position where the amount of Bitcoin leaving the market every day far exceeds the amount of new Bitcoin coming onto the market from miners and sellers.

B-Day is a term my friend Greg Cassar uses to describe the time in the not-too-distant future when there will be no more available Bitcoin supply on exchanges, but demand will remain constant or grow. This will cause rapid and exponential price appreciation of the type that the world has never seen before.

Similar to high-frequency trading using direct fibre optic connections, I believe that this is how any available Bitcoin will be purchased from exchanges and over-the-counter (OTC) trading in the near future. Any available Bitcoin supply will go to large institutions, nation states and ETFs, not retail investors like you and me.

The lesson is to buy and hold as much Bitcoin as you possibly can right now, as it will be your most valuable asset moving forward.

The Components of the Four-Year Bitcoin Cycle

"The history of Bitcoin trading is a bubble, a correction, consolidation, and another increase. It's happened four times, and it will happen again." – Barry Silbert, founder and CEO of Digital Currency Group

A Bitcoin cycle typically lasts for four years. Remember that past cycles and timings are no guarantee of future cycles, but based on history, the cycles repeat so similarly that they are a very good data point and trend to make informed decisions.

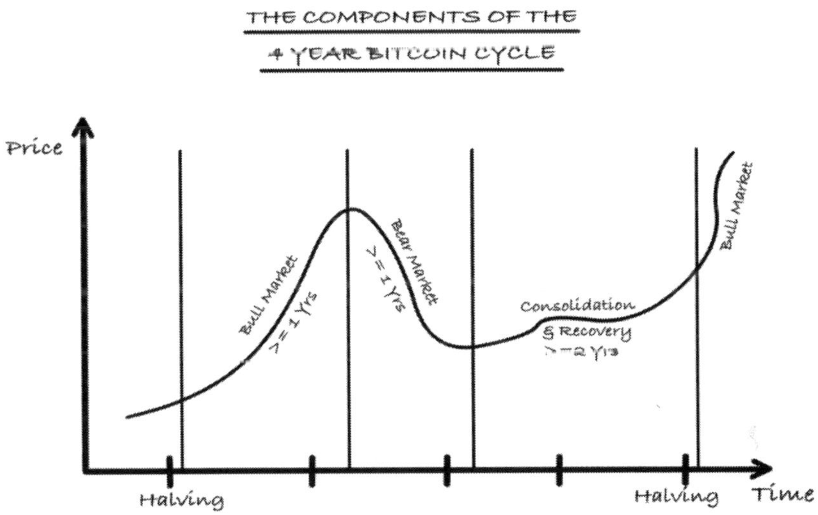

A halving event is historically followed by a bull market that often goes for a year or more.

This is then historically followed by a bear market for a year or more.

The market then slowly consolidates and recovers to the previous peak over approximately two years, before moving into the next bull market again.

I have just given you the key to building incredible wealth. If you understand this, you can start to time the market, buying at the bottom and selling at the top. We will cover this in greater detail in 'Chapter 7 – Millionaire Timing.'

What About Altcoins in the Cycle?

In terms of price appreciation in a bull market, Bitcoin usually experiences price gains first at the start of the cycle.

The high market cap Altcoins tend to rise in price in the following months and years.

Lower market cap Altcoins have historically been the last to pump, but because of the lower multiples, these experience the biggest gains when on a winner.

BITCOIN DRIVES THE MARKET

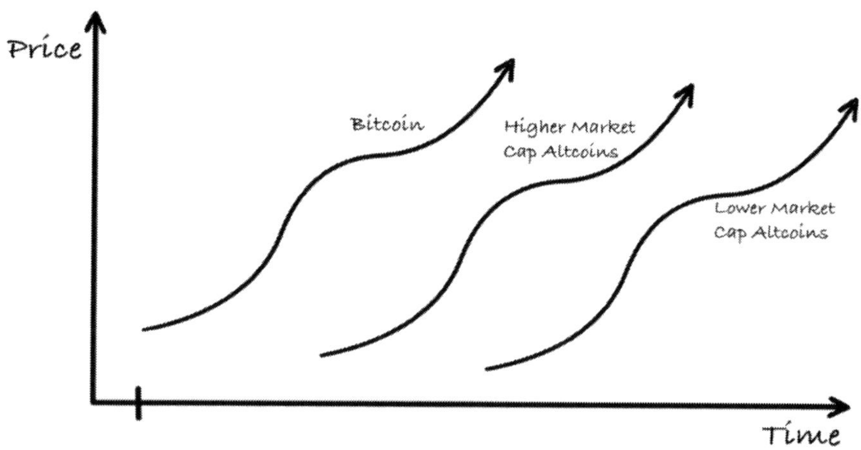

Chapter 5 – Winning Narratives Like a Millionaire

Second Component in The Crypto Pentagon Framework

This is the second component in the Crypto Pentagon Framework for winning the crypto game and joining the New Rich.

We started with learning the four-year cycle. Now, we will build on that by finding winning narratives.

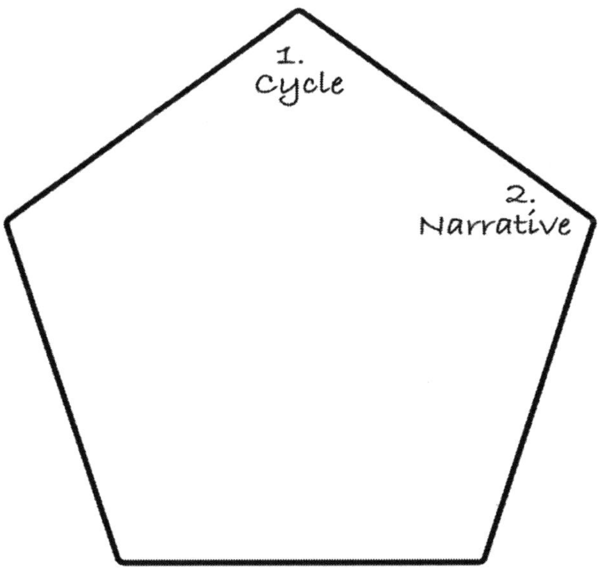

Win the Bull Run With Narratives

The crypto ecosystem is massive as it spans and is transforming finance, payments, stores of value, gaming, AI and many more industries. It's impossible to be an expert on every segment of the market.

When I first started in crypto, I was very technical and thought this was an advantage. I found through the 'School of Hard Knocks' that it wasn't about me, and it didn't matter what crypto projects I thought had the best solution or technology. None of this affected the price or demand at all.

Crypto asset growth within a market is about what the market is excited about. The market is excited about stories or narratives. You can think of this as themes within the overall crypto ecosystem.

Markets are driven by supply and demand and are largely influenced by 'group think.' So, the trick is to combine our preferences and gut feeling with what the market is excited about.

The stories that people pass from one to another control their focus, and where focus goes, the price flows.

Specialize in a Small Number of Narratives

Because the crypto industry is constantly evolving and growing, there are too many narratives for you to be an expert in all of them. Instead, we need to select a couple of narratives that we understand, are interested in, and that are popular with high growth potential.

By selecting and learning just a select number of popular narratives that you can relate to, you have a much greater chance of success. From my experience, two to four narratives are ideal to specialize in and invest within.

Examples of Popular Narratives

Popular narratives will change from cycle to cycle. They can also change within a cycle (we will go deeper into that coming up). This is by no means a definitive list of popular narratives, and this will change and get outdated over time. It represents some of the most popular narratives at the time of publishing of this book.

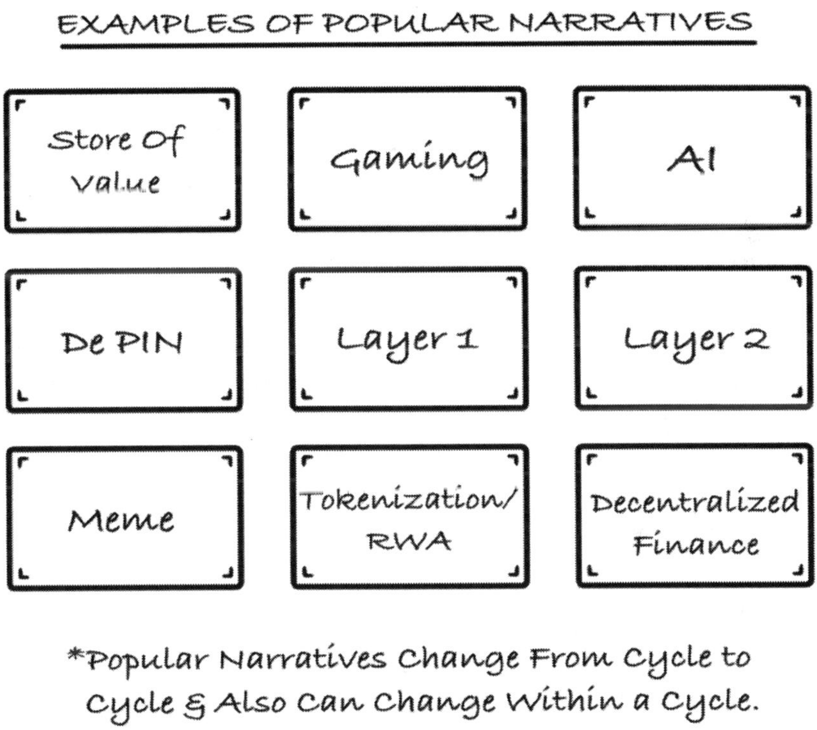

Choose Winning Narratives With the Triangulation Technique

The Triangulation Technique in investing typically involves using multiple data points or methods to confirm an investment decision.

By combining these different perspectives, we, as investors, can reduce the risk of relying on a single source of information and increase the likelihood of making informed decisions.

We can use the Triangulation Technique with narratives by identifying multiple respected authorities within the crypto industry and comparing the narratives they are most excited about.

See the example below. By studying and drawing conclusions from multiple data points, our chances of successfully picking the hottest narratives in a cycle increase significantly.

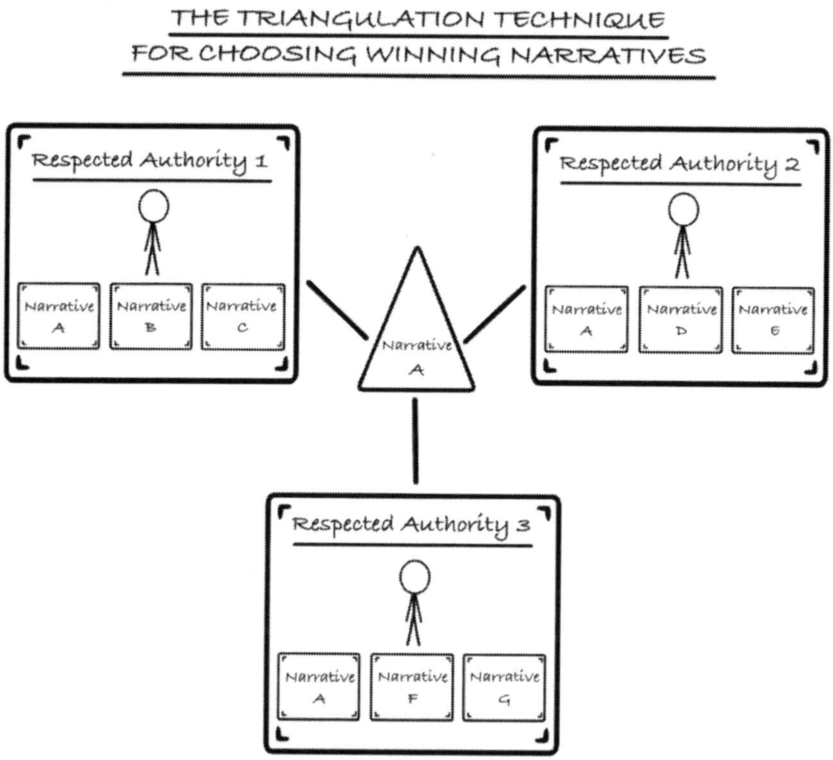

Narratives Cycle Timing

You will notice that within a market cycle, multiple narratives are being discussed and promoted. They won't all be hot in the market's minds simultaneously, and some narratives will hold the market's attention for longer than others.

When a narrative is being widely discussed, and excitement is generated about it, often the price of the projects within that narrative tends to move upward because of market speculation.

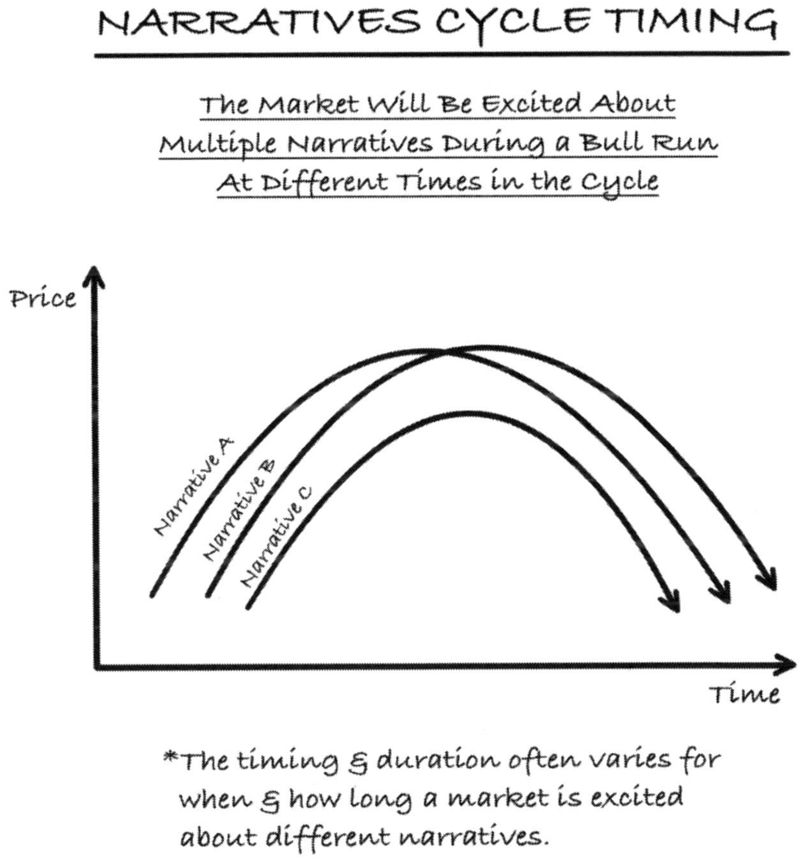

Pick The Winners Within Those Narratives

Once we have selected the narratives we will focus on and specialize in within a market cycle, the next step is choosing winning crypto projects within those narratives. Let's unpack that further in the next chapter as we move into portfolio design.

CHAPTER 6 – PROFITABLE PORTFOLIO DESIGN

SPECIAL OFFER TO GIVE YOU AN UNFAIR ADVANTAGE

Get the Video Training Course That Compliments This Book to Give You a Deeper Understanding of Winning Portfolio Design & Asset Allocation, So That You Can Maximize Your Opportunities in the Current Market.

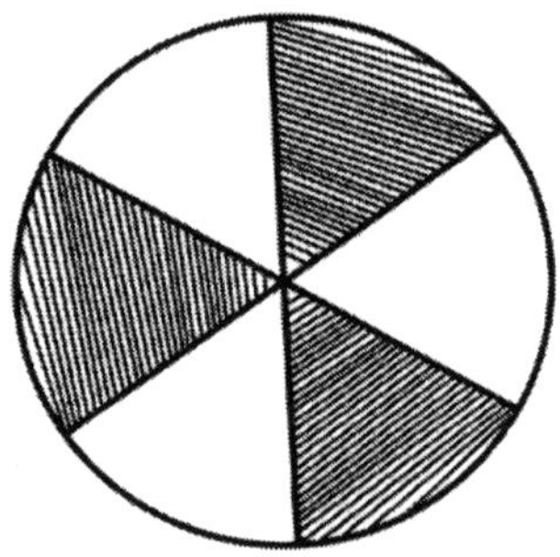

See CryptoNewRich.com/portfolio

**The above-listed investment in your education is risk-free, as we offer a 100% money-back guarantee. In the unlikely event that you have watched the training and did not get amazing value from it, just reach out to our team, and we will refund your money in full.*

Third Component in The Crypto Pentagon Framework

This is the third component in the Crypto Pentagon Framework for winning the crypto game and joining the New Rich.

We started by learning the four-year cycle. Then, we built on that by finding winning narratives. We now need to design a winning portfolio that is consistent with our narratives. The portfolio should reduce our risk while also being designed to achieve exciting growth.

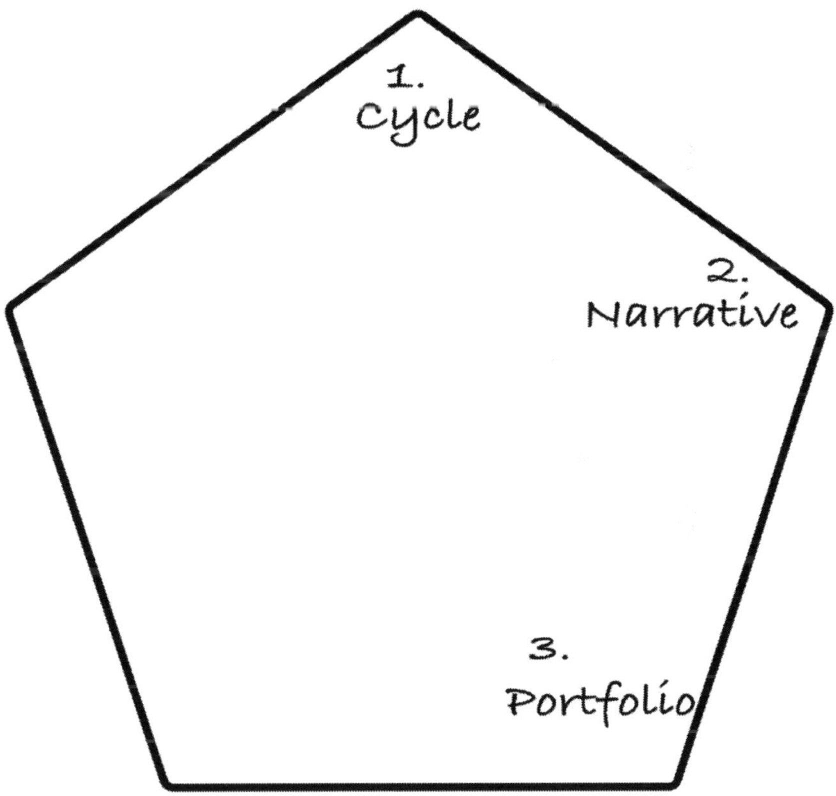

The World's Easiest Wealth Creation Portfolio With Crypto – Stacking SATs

"Annualized return of Bitcoin is 140% a year since 2012. You can own any VC fund, any asset class, nothing comes close. 20 Million percent returns since 2012." – Raoul Pal

In the Bitcoin Essentials section, we discussed Satoshis (SATS) and the fact that there are 100 million SATS in one Bitcoin.

People often think, *"I'm not going to buy a Bitcoin because I can't afford to buy a whole one,"* but we don't have to. You can buy SATS, which are a fraction of a Bitcoin, e.g. 0.05 BTC.

A common way of getting very wealthy over time is accumulating Bitcoin. Continually keep stacking SATS.

This strategy works by buying more Bitcoin whenever you get paid. Whenever you get any extra money in, you buy some more Bitcoin. Stacking SATS is really the easiest and simplest investment strategy with crypto.

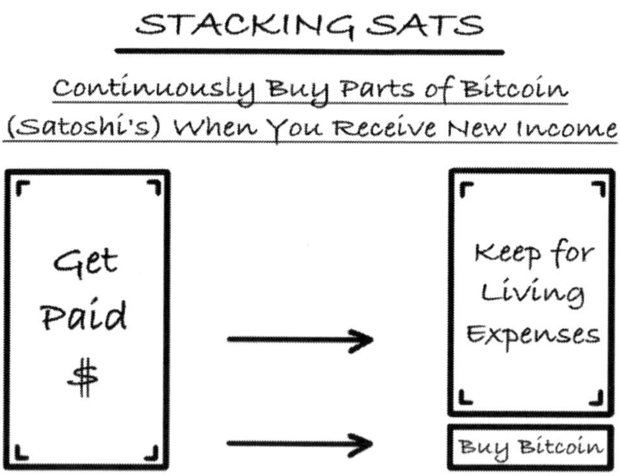

In the scenario above, we get paid from our job or business and we buy some Bitcoin. We don't put our whole wage into it because we

need to keep money for living expenses, fun, and some financial reserves.

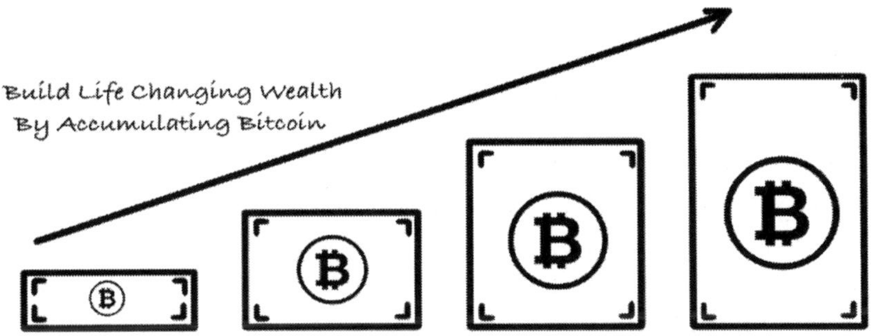

Over time, you can build life-changing wealth by stacking SATS because you keep adding to your bag of Bitcoin. Remember, the Bitcoin price has historically been rising consistently. So, as you accumulate more, it's building up like an exponential curve. You are adding more to your bag, and its value is increasing over and over and over again.

VC Theory Portfolio

In the 2017 crypto bull run, my primary focus was accumulating Bitcoin. I wasn't focused on Altcoins at all. Back then, I thought it wasn't clear who the 'long-term winners' were other than Bitcoin.

A good friend of mine, Kevin Mendoza, who was very smart and taught me so much about becoming a crypto multi-millionaire, advised me that he thought I was leaving a lot of money on the table by not thinking like a venture capitalist (VC).

VCs place multiple investments, knowing that some will have incredible returns, some of them will do just OK, and others will make no money or lose money. The idea is that the exponential winners pull up the portfolio's results.

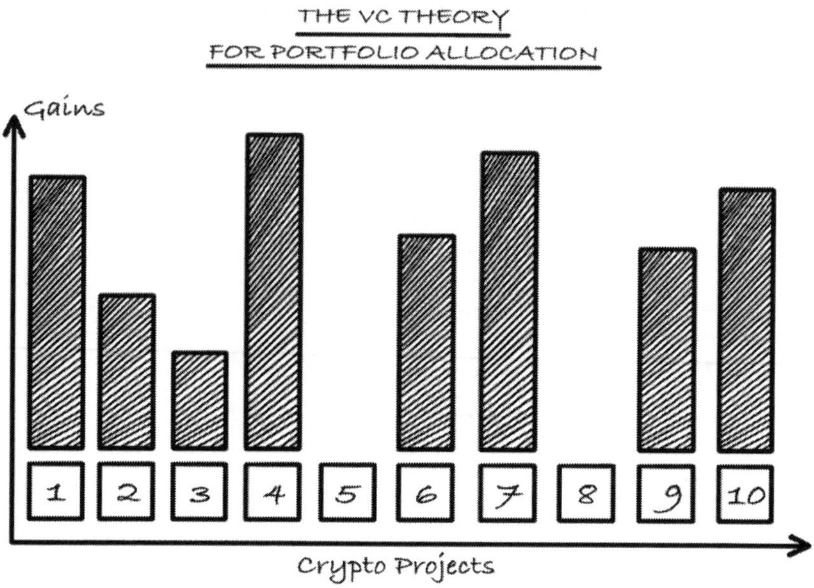

We can see in this example above that some of the crypto projects got exponential results, while others didn't do very well at all. The winner's results far outweighed the loser's losses.

The VC theory really changed the portfolio growth that I got over time. You will see how this becomes even more powerful when we get into the sections on Timing and Multiple cycles coming up.

Avoid These Two Common Crypto Portfolio Problems

Let's now look at two very common crypto portfolio problems you should work to avoid. I consistently see these problems when talking to less experienced investors who are leaving money on the table or taking more risks than they need to.

The first one is that there are too few crypto projects. In this portfolio design, the investor is not diversified enough. If you only have three or four crypto projects and one of them doesn't perform, or two of them don't work, then that really could be a major hit, with as much as 25 or 50% of your portfolio not doing well. So, we want to avoid that.

The other one that I see often is too many crypto projects. I have a friend who has invested in 170 crypto projects. In this situation, no individual project has enough capital. When a project gets on a run, say it goes up 5x or 10x, it doesn't really move the needle on your total portfolio value much because it's not a large number that is being multiplied (as the investments are spread too thin).

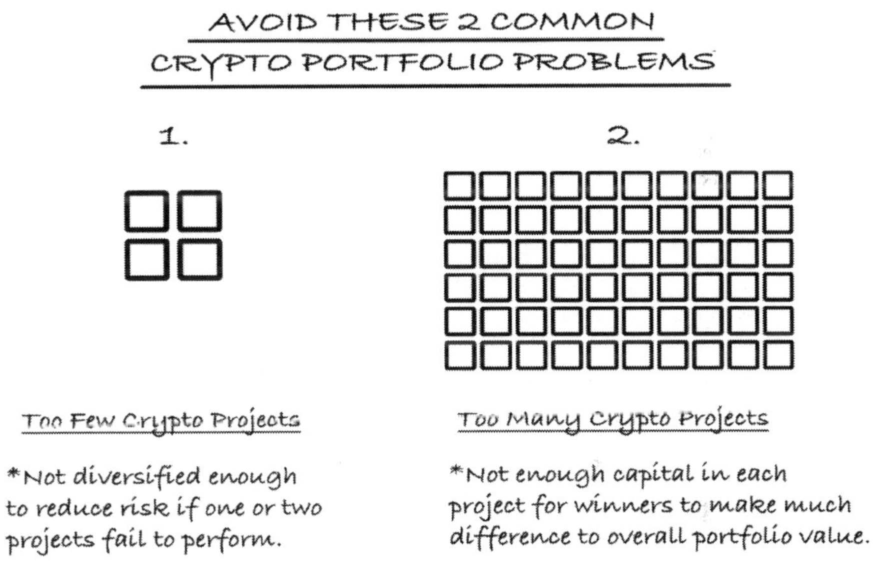

From experience, I have found that ideally between 10 and 30 crypto projects in your portfolio as we lead into a bull market can be great.

If you've invested a smaller amount of money, like $10K, then 10 projects could be good because you'll be able to move the needle a little bit if you get on a winner.

But say you are in the tens of thousands or hundreds of thousands or into the millions of dollars invested. A larger number of investments of up to around 30 could work for really spreading the risk and finding more winners. But there are big enough bets so that if you get on a winner, you can really run it long and multiply large numbers.

Criteria For Consideration When Selecting Crypto Projects to Invest In

When considering investing in crypto projects, we must ask, *What are the criteria for choosing our investments? How are we going to decide on winning projects?'*

Ideally, the investments you choose should meet multiple of these criteria. This list is by no means exhaustive; it's designed to be simple and give you a framework to consider these decisions.

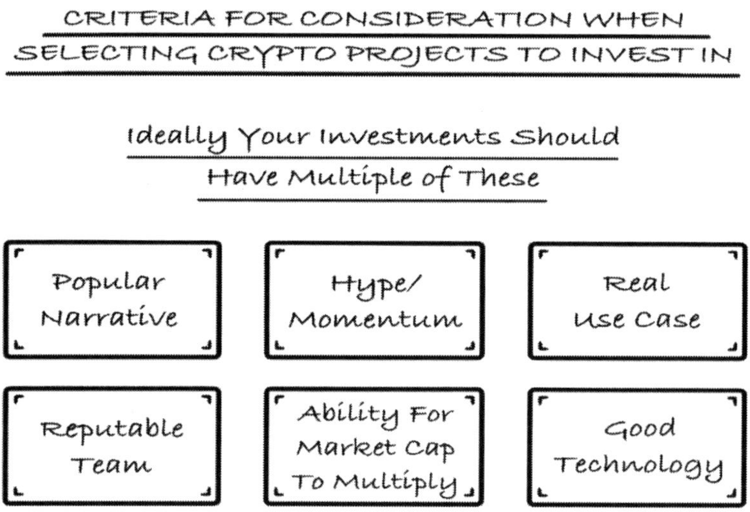

Effectively, we need to consider these things when deciding on crypto projects to invest in…

- Is the crypto project in a populated narrative that the market is excited about?
- Is there hype and momentum surrounding the crypto project? Is there a buzz about it? Are VCs excited about it and backing it?
- We don't want it to be vaporware. Does the project have a real use case? Is anyone using this for anything real?
- Are their team doxed? Meaning, have they revealed their identity? Do they have a real history? Have they come from a

corporate background? Have they come from a cryptography background? Are they from a finance background? Are they a reputable team? Do they have a track record of success before? Have they built other businesses?

- Is the market cap low? Are there other similar projects with a higher market cap that this one could catch up to? Is there room for the market cap to multiply?
- Lastly, does it have good technology? Are other winning projects using similar technology?

Choose Winning Projects with the Triangulation Technique

Just like we did when we looked at narratives, we now have the triangulation technique that we can apply when selecting crypto projects with a high chance of winning.

By combining these different perspectives, we, as investors, can reduce the risk of relying on a single source of information and increase the likelihood of making informed decisions.

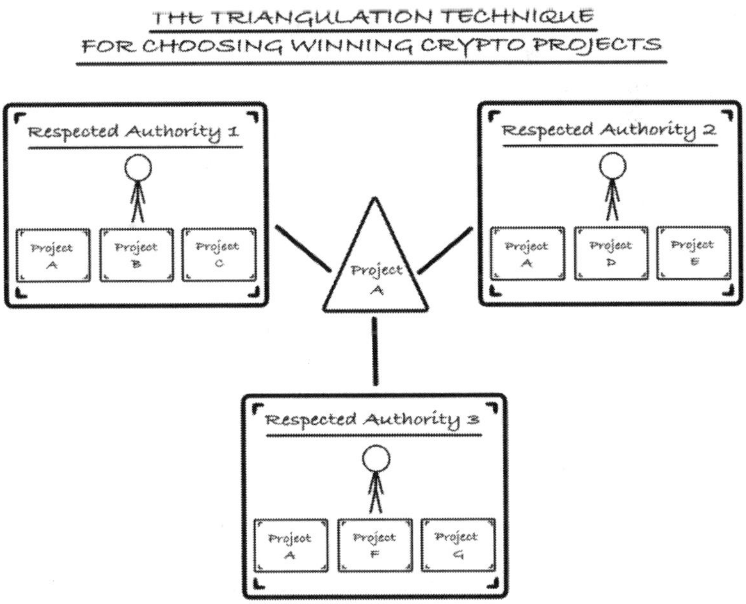

Do Your Own Research

"We live in a world where knowledge is power, and those who have the information and insights will have the advantage." – Cathie Wood, American investor and founder, CEO and CIO of Ark Invest

One way to gain a competitive advantage is to always do your own research when selecting projects for your portfolio. This can involve reading the founders' white papers by the founders or the crypto project's website.

Another two techniques for doing your own research include following the crypto project or its founders on X (formerly Twitter) and watching multiple YouTube videos on the subject to get a balanced view and make more informed decisions. It perplexes me when people have thousands, sometimes tens and hundreds of thousands and even millions of dollars in crypto projects that they have absolutely no idea about.

A Winning Portfolio Strategy

Below is an example of a very common and successful portfolio strategy. It combines safe, low-risk, and high-risk investments.

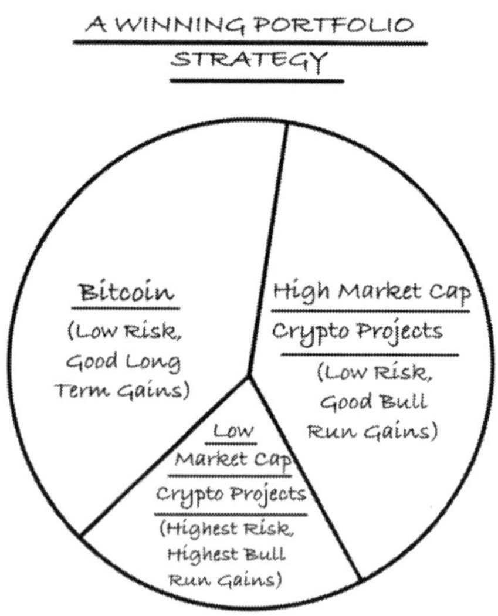

The first investment into a crypto portfolio is often Bitcoin for the following reasons. It is…

- The first crypto currency.
- The biggest global brand name.
- Considered the safest crypto investment.
- The most proven in terms of security.
- Proven to have a large track record of gains over a long period.
- Experiencing exponential global demand.

This portfolio structure is then complimented with 'high market cap crypto projects.' These are often projects in the top 50 when ranked by market cap. Portfolio considerations include:

- More proven technology.
- Less risk of failure.
- High demand for these projects globally.
- Good track record of gains over a bull market or long period.

The smallest component in this portfolio structure is 'low market cap crypto projects.' These are often projects below the top 50 when ranked by market cap. Portfolio considerations include:

- A low market cap means less capital is required for multiples in price.
- Higher risk of failure on individual projects, but this can be offset by larger gains on other projects.
- Get access to a project early in their lifecycle for longer-term higher multiples.

A Higher-Risk Portfolio Strategy for Those with Less Capital Seeking Faster Gains

"The biggest risk is not taking any risk. In a world that is changing quickly, the only strategy that is guaranteed to fail is not taking risks." – Cathie Wood

If you have a smaller amount of money to invest or seek faster gains, a higher-risk portfolio strategy would be to have a much smaller percentage of Bitcoin in your portfolio. Even though it will do well in the long term, in the bull run, it won't grow as fast as some of the Altcoins.

In this portfolio structure, you may have a lower percentage allocation than the previous portfolio in high market cap crypto projects and, instead, go for a higher weighting in the lower market cap crypto projects.

This portfolio design has a higher degree of risk associated with it. If you think back to our VC strategy, we acknowledge that some of the investments could go to zero. In this high-risk portfolio, the investor is willing to take on that risk because some projects may end up as 10x, 20x, or even a 50x winner. It doesn't take many winners like that to change the math of your portfolio's growth.

A HIGHER RISK PORTFOLIO STRATEGY
FOR THOSE WITH LESS CAPITAL
WHO ARE SEEKING FASTER GAINS

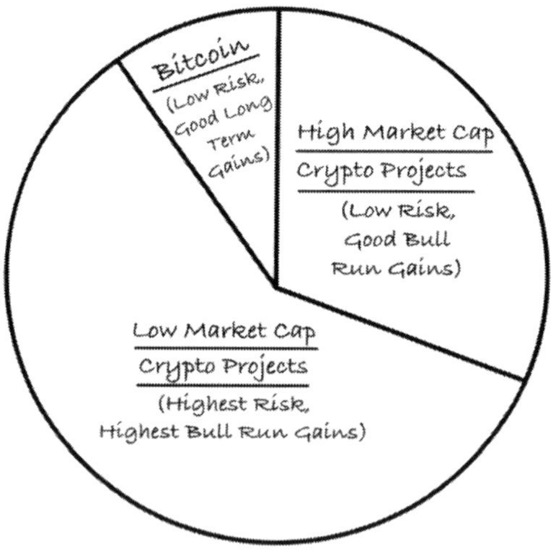

I've been low on cash many times, so I get it – we all want to get out of that situation as fast as possible. One of the things I'm trying to get across in this book and associated video training is the 'multi-cycle wealth mentality.'

I get it that no one wants to hear that they should string together multiple cycles to build generational wealth, but it's similar in concept to wanting to build muscle without consistently lifting weights over a period of time.

With low market cap crypto projects, like any investment, only put in what you are willing to lose.

Move With Speed on New High Conviction Projects

One of the ways that I've sometimes really gotten ahead was by selecting winning narratives and then following the progress of new, exciting, hyped projects that were coming up.

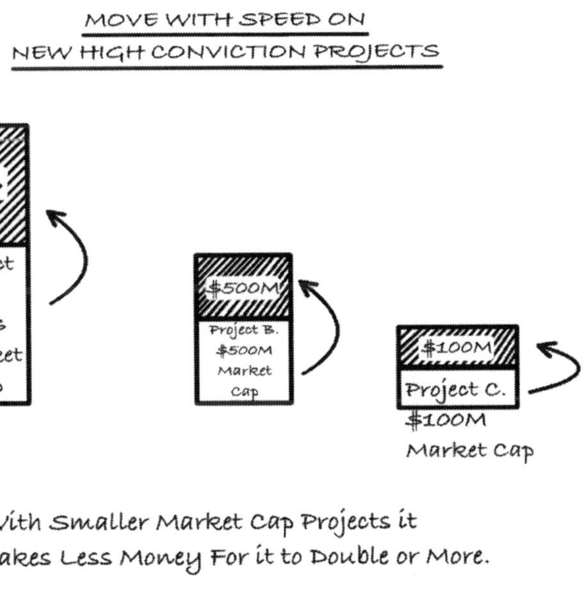

It can be powerful to move quickly on new high-conviction projects. Based on our triangulation method, if there's a hot narrative and then a new project with a lot of excitement and hype around it, sometimes it makes sense to move quickly on that investment.

The reason is that smaller market cap projects require less capital to invest in for their prices to double or more.

In our example above, if we have project A with a $1 billion market cap, we would need to invest another billion dollars of capital in it to double in price.

If we had a $500M market cap for project B, it would only need another $500M to double in price.

If project C was a newer project that we quickly invested in because of its $100M market cap, it would only take $100M to come into it for it to double in price.

If project C got $1 billion to go into it, that's when it would be 10x in price, and things get exciting quickly. With this technique, many investors have changed their financial lives in as little as one bull market.

Feed the Beast

'Feed the beast' is a term that I use to describe the concept of investing new capital into the market consistently at strategic times rather than just investing once and waiting for the gains to happen.

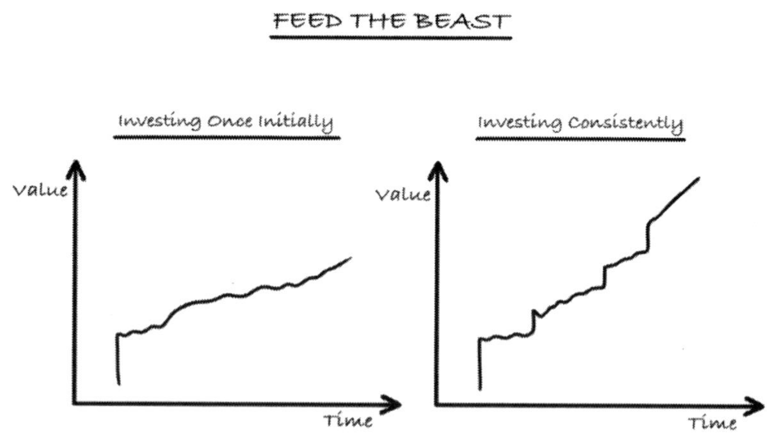

I've got a good friend, Brian, who once received a large chunk of money. He put it into the market, and is a smart investor who did well, but then he didn't want to work to produce additional income to complement his gains.

Now, my portfolio is more than double the size of Brian's, even though he started initially with more money invested than me. I've been working hard for additional income streams and consistently feeding the beast through the bear market and the bottom of the bull market.

The diagram above shows that the investor who is consistently investing gets small bumps in portfolio size. While this doesn't seem like much, it does make a massive difference over time, especially when projects get on a winning run and achieve a high multiple. You could imagine $15K invested if it achieved a 10x is more exciting at $150K, than $10K if we didn't feed the beast for the same 10x, only producing $100K. In that hypothetical example, there is only a $5K difference in input and a $50K difference in the result.

You'll find that the results you'll get from 'Feeding the beast' will far exceed the ones you will get if you just invest once.

Feeding the beast will allow you to take fewer risks and exit the bull market earlier and safer. Say, for example, you put $10K in initially, and your goal was, *'I need to get to $100K by the end of the bull run'*. If you don't feed the beast, you will need to achieve a 10x on your portfolio to achieve your goal.

If you were able to feed the beast another $10K over time, then now you only need to achieve a 5x on your money (based on $20K invested) to achieve your $100K goal.

This may allow you to exit the bull market earlier, which is much safer. We will discuss this in more depth in Chapter 7 on Timing. Feeding the beast is a very important strategy for your investing success.

Periodically Rebalancing Portfolio

You will find is that over time, and especially in bull market conditions, we have projects in our VC portfolio strategy that are not performing well.

One of the ways that I get massive growth is to look at it every couple of months and then rebalance the portfolio. Rebalancing the portfolio means, *'Let's take money that was allocated here, but it's not performing, and re-allocate those funds into the projects that are really moving forward and growing.'*

So, we sell underperforming assets and re-allocate the funds to higher-performing assets or buy new assets with momentum and conviction.

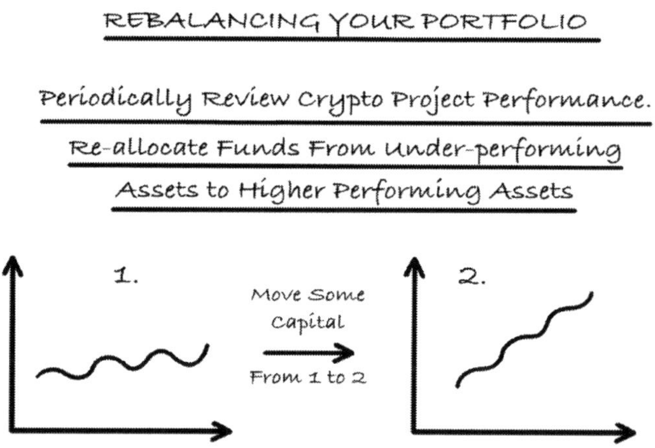

In this example, crypto project 1 is slowly increasing, but it's not moving much. Crypto project 2 has been growing well. The market's excited about crypto project 2, and we believe that it has the potential for more growth.

So, we move some or all the capital from project 1 to project 2, and then the same thing here from project 3 to project 4.

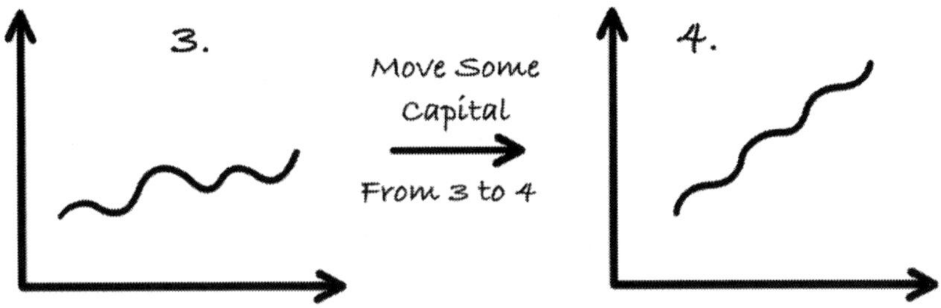

You may need to do this multiple times through a market cycle to ensure that all projects in your portfolio are growing well.

Putting It All Together

It really makes a difference if you can use this portfolio rebalancing strategy and feed the beast.

If you can get a combination of your VC portfolio and stacking SATS, you are really starting to win the game.

In the next chapter, we will cover Market Timing. When do we get in? When do we get out? How do the actual market cycles work?

Chapter 7 – Timing for Maximum Profits

Fourth Component in The Crypto Pentagon Framework

This is the fourth component in the Crypto Pentagon Framework for winning the crypto game and joining the New Rich.

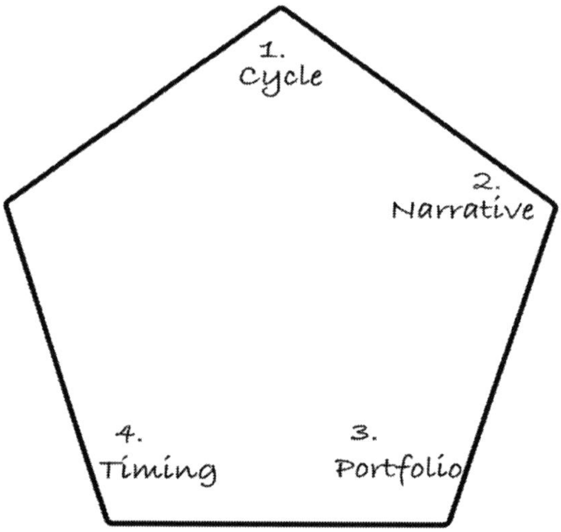

The Crystal Ball and History

"History doesn't repeat itself, but it does rhyme." – Mark Twain, American writer, humorist and essayist

With timing the market, everyone wants to know when it will go up, when it will go down, when to enter and when to exit the market.

Unfortunately, no one has a crystal ball and knows exactly what markets will do and when.

What we can do is learn from what has happened and at what time in previous market cycles. This allows us to make informed decisions and educated guesses to help stack the odds of success in our favour.

There is never a guarantee that this next market cycle will behave exactly like the previous cycle or cycles. Still, by studying multiple cycles, we can draw meaningful conclusions that will help point us in the right direction.

Continual Learning So You Can Adjust Strategy if Breaking Away From the Cycle

"Most people want to change their circumstances to improve their lives, instead of changing themselves to improve their circumstances." – John C Maxwell, American author and speaker

Every day, I use sources such as X (formerly Twitter) and YouTube to continually educate myself on what is happening with the market, the cycle, the US economy (as it affects crypto the most), laws and individual projects.

I use this information to supplement my understanding of the previous market cycles because I'm always looking to see if the world has changed and how it could change how previous market cycles have behaved.

A good example is the introduction of the Bitcoin ETFs in the US. This added significant global demand for Bitcoin and upward price action. At the end of a bull market cycle, I would not expect Bitcoin to have as dramatic drawbacks in price as it did when it was mainly just retail investors driving the market. However, with the biggest financial institutions in the world now having access to profit from Bitcoin's price action, we need to be prepared for anything and everything.

I recommend you continually do your research and look out for changes that can affect the markets, as in the example above. Also, be prepared to adapt to the market. Don't ever be married to any one strategy. Yes, the market historically is telling us this right now, but if that data ever changes, we need to be ready to adapt and change with that. If there's one thing that I learned very early on with markets, the market most certainly doesn't care about your feelings. If the data and sentiment change over time, you better be ready to adapt to that. If you don't, the market will simply chew you up and spit you out.

One of the most respected market cycle experts I know, Bob Loukas, says this, *"I draw multiple paths on charts, because I learned a long time ago believing in one (biased) path led to disappointment."*

Quick Recap of the Four-Year Cycle

Looking at the previous four-year cycles for Bitcoin is our best guide. We covered this previously, but here is a quick recap so it's fresh in your mind as we dive deeper into timings.

THE COMPONENTS OF THE 4 YEAR BITCOIN CYCLE

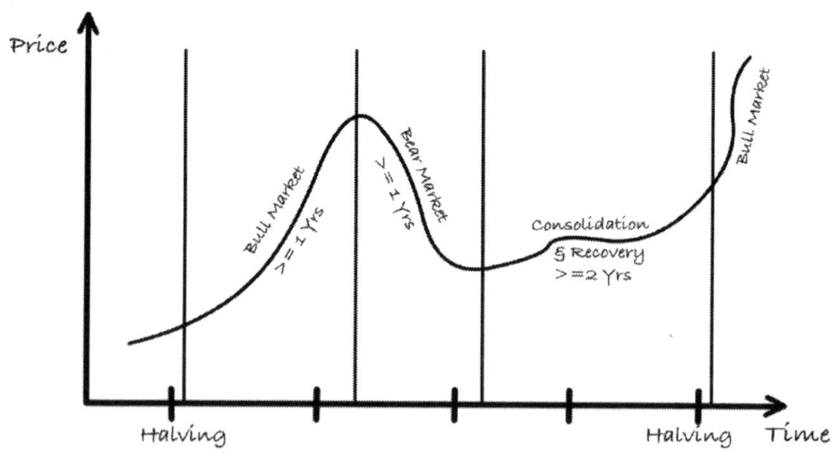

Historically, a halving event is almost immediately followed by a bull market that often lasts a year or more.

This is then historically followed by a bear market for a year or more.

Historically, the market has slowly consolidated and recovered to its previous peak across approximately two years before moving into the next bull market again.

Crypto Seasons

Everyone wants to make money right now. I think of markets as like a farmer. The farmer wants crops to sell right now, but it doesn't work like that – he/she needs to learn the seasons and understand when to plant, let it grow, and harvest.

If we think about the crypto market like seasons for a farmer. See the diagram below to see a full cycle.

We are selling/harvesting off last season's crop at the top of the bull market.

Then, we patiently wait until the bear market, and plant/buy at the bottom when no one else wants to buy.

Once we have planted our seeds, we must let them grow.

For our grow season, we will add to our positions with the 'Feed the beast' strategy as the market rises into and through the early stages of the bull market.

Then we'll harvest/sell again to complete a full cycle of crypto seasons.

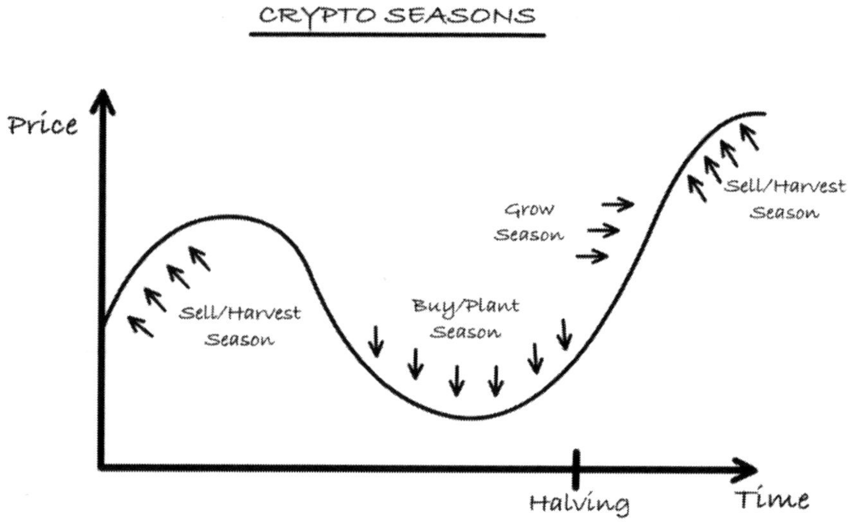

Buy When Everyone Else is Selling and Be Counter-Cyclical to the Masses

"The time to buy is when there's blood in the streets." – Baron Rothschild, British Peer, investment banker and member of the Rothschild banking family

Ultimately, we want to be countercyclical to everyone else. We want to buy when everyone else is selling and sell when everyone else is buying. This is how real wealth is made, especially when compounded over multiple cycles (we will cover this in-depth in the next chapter).

You can see in the diagram below that the fearful investors are selling and exiting the market because the news would be all doom and gloom in the world and in crypto.

Expert investors understand the market cycles and, at the exact same time, are buying the market correction.

BUY WHEN EVERYONE ELSE IS SELLING

The diagram below shows that most people only want to buy in the bull market when the prices increase. While gains can be had then, the real gains are made by the expert investors who are buying in the bear market.

THE 4 YEAR BITCOIN CYCLE

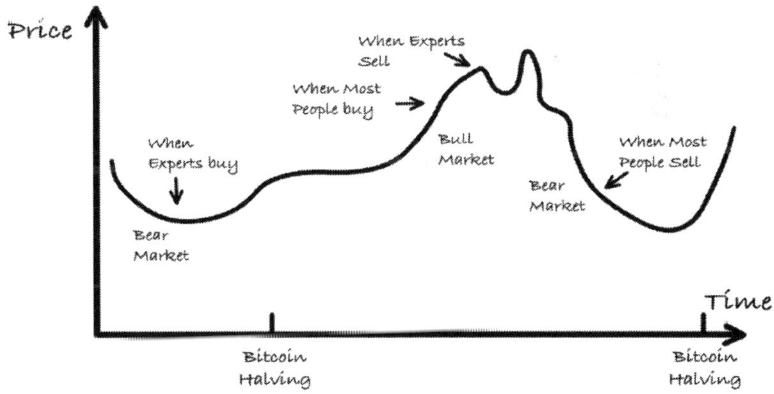

Expert investors study previous cycles to understand the market timings and exit earlier, near the bull market's top. Most people don't understand the market cycle timings and hold on for more gains, only to ride it back down to the bottom and sell at the worst time.

No One Ever Went Broke From Taking Profits

You don't want to ride the market up only to ride it back down again. It hurts. How do I know? Because I've made that mistake in the past, and so has nearly every other investor on their journey.

A famous proverb says: *'A bird in the hand is worth two in the bush.'* This means it is better to be content with what you have than risk losing everything by seeking more.

No one ever went broke from taking profits, so if you are happy with your gains or recognize that you have had significant gains, please don't be shy to exit some positions or parts of some positions to take some profits and remove your risk.

Dry Powder Ready to Deploy

"The true investors make more when markets crash." – Robert Kiyosaki, American businessman and author of the *Rich Dad Poor Dad* book series

Venture capitalists often use the term 'dry powder' to refer to cash reserves that are ready for them to deploy quickly when an opportunity arises.

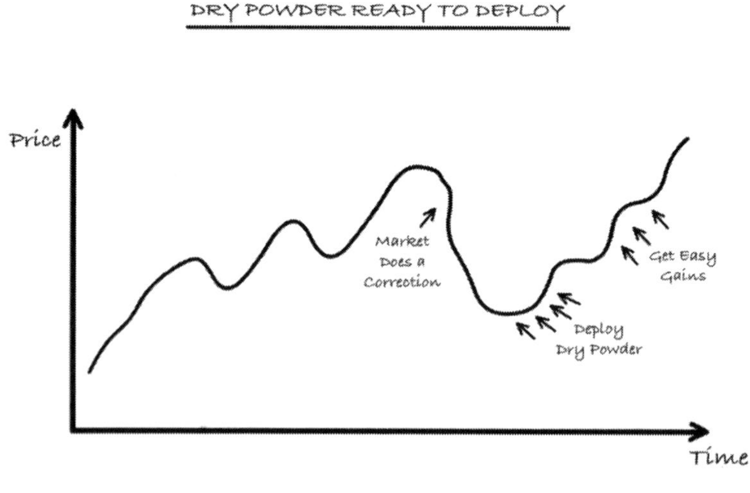

Large market players constantly manipulate the markets or use the media to manipulate them so that people get fearful and sell, thus giving themselves better buying opportunities.

If you have dry powder cash reserves in your bank account or on your exchanges ready to deploy, you can watch out for large market corrections and buy the dips when you see early signs that it is turning around again.

The trick is to have the dry powder cash sitting there. I have been guilty many times of having deployed all my capital into the markets and not having spare cash ready to roll. Somehow, I don't think I'm alone on that one, especially in an upward market like a bull market.

Roughly Get the Top & the Bottom of the Market With Dollar Cost Averaging

It's very hard to pick the exact bottom of a market cycle to enter a buying position or the exact top of a market cycle to exit a position.

As we learned earlier, the term 'dollar cost averaging' refers to spreading your investments over multiple time periods, such as weeks or months, to average out your buy or sell position. The goal is to roughly buy the bottom or sell the top of a market cycle.

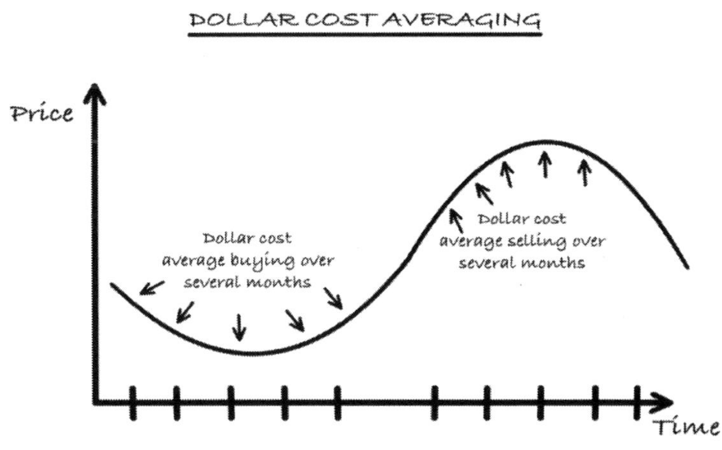

This approach, combined with what we have been learning about market timings, gives you a far greater chance of achieving your investing goals than if you were to do all your buying or exiting of the market at one point.

What Positions to Exit or Hold at the Top of the Market

By studying the previous four-year cycles, we can see that during the bear market, both Bitcoin and the Altcoins have experienced dramatic pullbacks in price from their bull market 'all-time highs.'

While Bitcoin is still expected to make price adjustments, following the introduction of the Bitcoin ETFs, it is unlikely that it will see dramatic pullbacks like it has in the past because most of the buyers are long-term holders.

I expect that Altcoins will still do dramatic price declines during bear markets, as shown below.

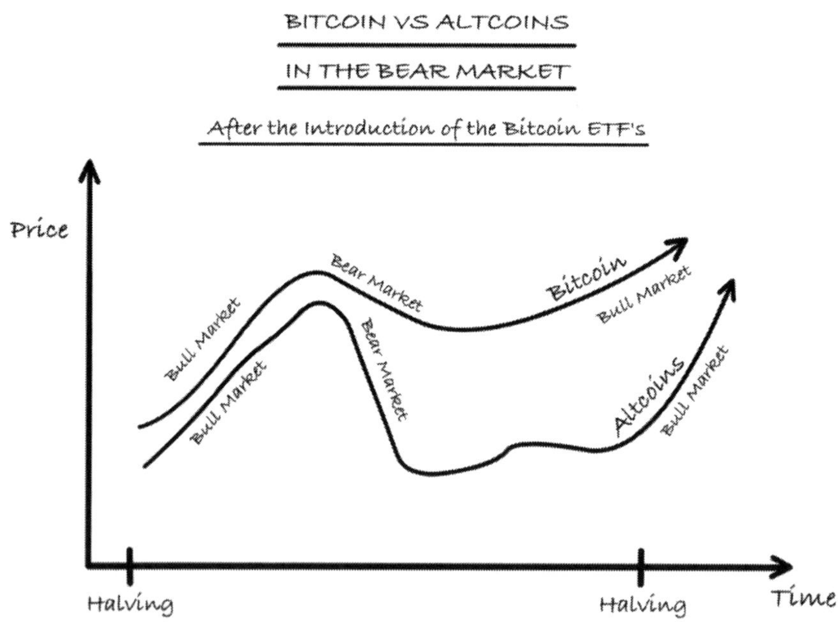

This brings us to the question of the best strategy at the end of a bull market cycle.

My strategy is simple. The goal should always be 'Stacking SATS' (accumulating Bitcoin). I hold Bitcoin long-term through both the bull market and into the bear market. However, the percentage of Bitcoin in my portfolio decreases as I'm buying quality long-term Altcoins at the bottom of the market. I then aim to sell my Altcoins at the top of the market, to, in turn, accumulate even more Bitcoin (staking SATS). The ultimate aim here is to always accumulate more and more Bitcoins across multiple cycles.

As shown in the diagram below, I will sell Altcoins toward the top of the bull market and then buy back in again as close as I get to the bottom of the bear market. I'm seeking Altcoins that will outperform Bitcoin in the upcoming bull market cycle. I can buy back into Bitcoin at the bottom of the cycle and have more Bitcoins than at the top of the previous cycle.

HOLD OR EXIT POSITIONS

AT THE TOP OF THE BULL MARKET

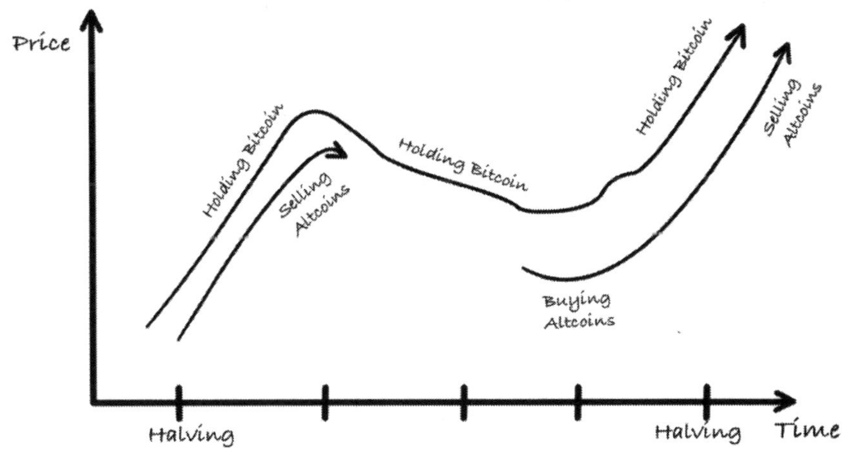

THE 2 RISKS WHEN PLANNING TO EXIT THE BULL MARKET

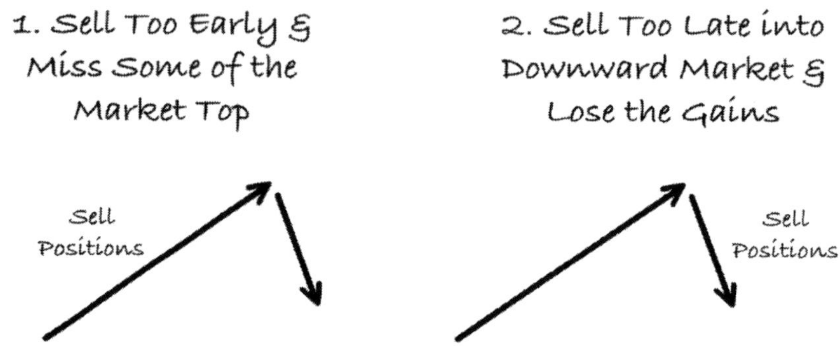

The diagram above shows the real balancing act that investors need to deal with when exiting their positions. If we sell too early, we feel like we have left some money on the table and we may feel foolish for getting the timing wrong. If we sell too late, the market will adjust downwards, and we will lose some of our gains.

Based on experience, I can advise that it is much better to get out early rather than late. The reason why is twofold. The first reason is that if we leave the market early, we are still leaving in profit. The second reason is that if we are selling into a downward market, there may not be the liquidity of buyers wanting to buy our selling positions (meaning that we can't get out of the market).

Zoom Out For Perspective

"Troy, crypto is down again this week, aren't you worried? What's going on?" – I have people in my life who say this to me regularly as the market does its normal price adjustments.

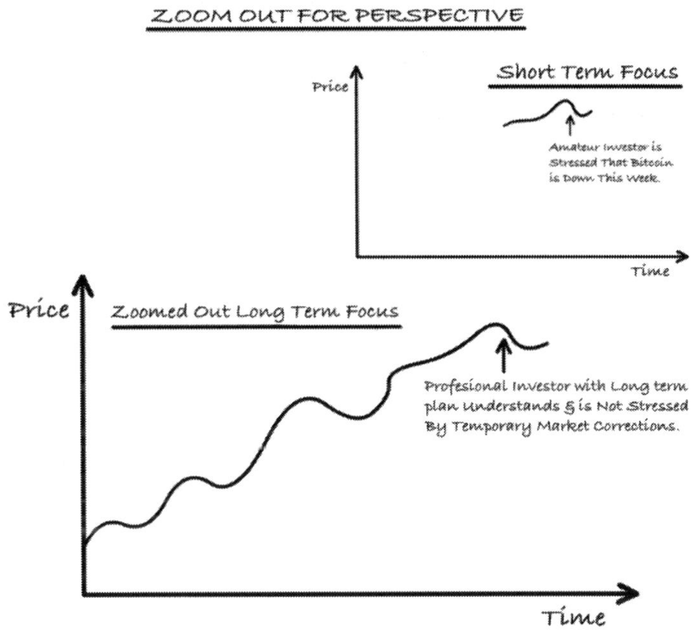

I have found that people who are concerned about day-to-day and week-to-week pricing don't have a long-term focus. They are thinking about this week, this month and *'How can I get rich this year?'* Many of these people also lack the emotional intelligence it takes to be a good investor.

Winners in crypto have a long-term strategy; they zoom out to see the big picture and see if they are 'directionally correct' with how the market is moving (they have made investments that are trending up and to the right). Winners remove all emotions and stick to the long-term plan. These price corrections rather than being something to be stressed about could be an opportunity to buy the dip with our spare dry powder.

This brings us to our next chapter of how real wealth is made: 'Multiple Cycles for Maximum Profits.'

Chapter 8 – Multiple Cycles For Maximum Profits

SPECIAL OFFER TO GIVE YOU AN UNFAIR ADVANTAGE

Get the Video Training Course That Compliments This Book to Give You a Deeper Understanding of the Current Market Cycles, So That You Can Make Good Decisions on When to Enter & Exit the Market.

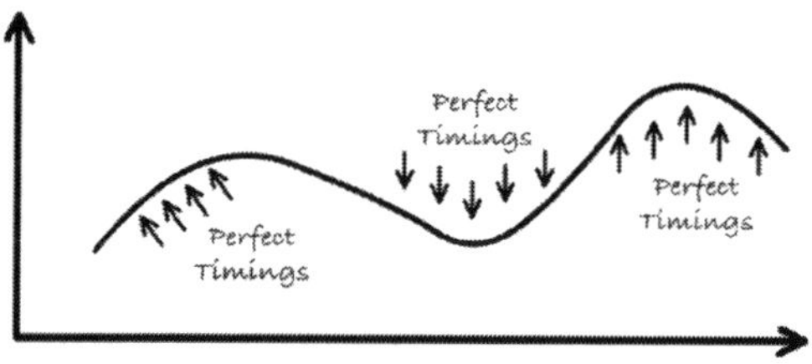

See CryptoNewRich.com/cycles

**The above-listed investment in your education IS RISK-FREE, as we offer a 100% money-back guarantee. In the unlikely event that you have watched the training and did not get amazing value from it, just reach out to our team, and we will refund your money in full.*

Fifth Component in The Crypto Pentagon Framework

This is the fifth component in the Crypto Pentagon Framework for winning the crypto game and joining the New Rich.

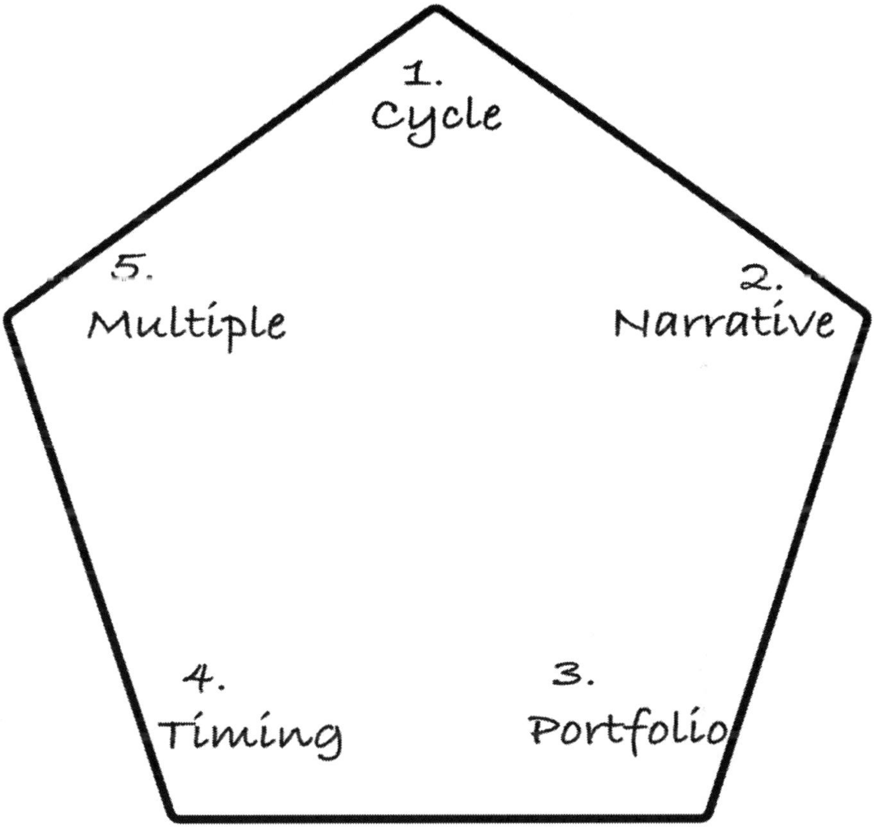

You Need to Cycle

"You make your money by the waiting." – Charlie Munger

Everyone wants to be a millionaire right now. Decide if you are going to be an amateur or a professional. I have this saying: *"You need to cycle."* This means that you need to experience a full four-year cycle to learn from it and set yourself up for future cycle success.

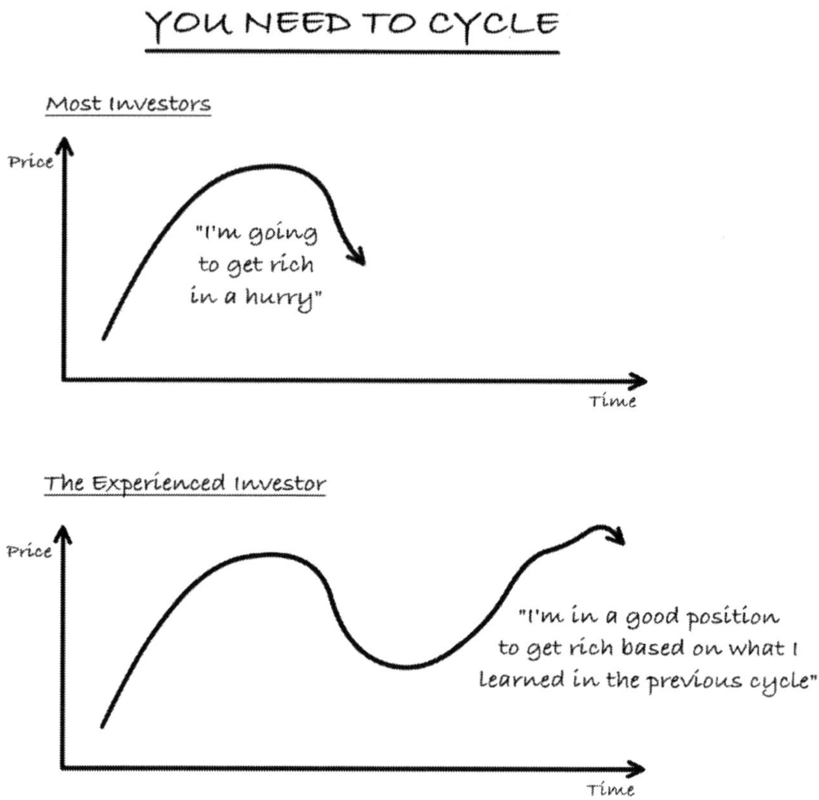

We need to go through a bear market, a bull market, and the sideways chop just to get that experience and the feeling. Then, when it comes up again, you will be able to think and know, '*I remember this; it's normal.*' Hold the course and make good, informed investment decisions.

Think in Multiple Four-Year Cycles

Most people are very short-term focused and can't think beyond where they are right now.

As much as 80% of success is mindset. We need to transition our mindset from *"I'm going to get wealthy in this bull market"* to *"I am willing to play the long game over 8 to 12 years to set myself and my family up for life."*

It's not a popular opinion, I do understand. What next? I'll be asking you to eat your vegetables and do exercise. Why hasn't someone just invented a pill for that?

Zoom Out & Play the Long Game

I have lots of friends who are crypto millionaires and multi-millionaires. I don't know any of them that got to 'generational wealth' in their first market cycle. I don't know any of them who didn't make mistakes in their first four-year cycle.

Everyone wants to get rich in a hurry. While this can happen in crypto, it's more likely that you will earn some good gains in your first cycle. Still, the real thing you will gain is knowledge and wisdom to set yourself up for incredible life-changing gains in your second and third cycles.

The two diagrams below show the difference between the game most investors are playing and the game of the experienced, knowledgeable investor. I'm playing the second game. Which one are you playing?

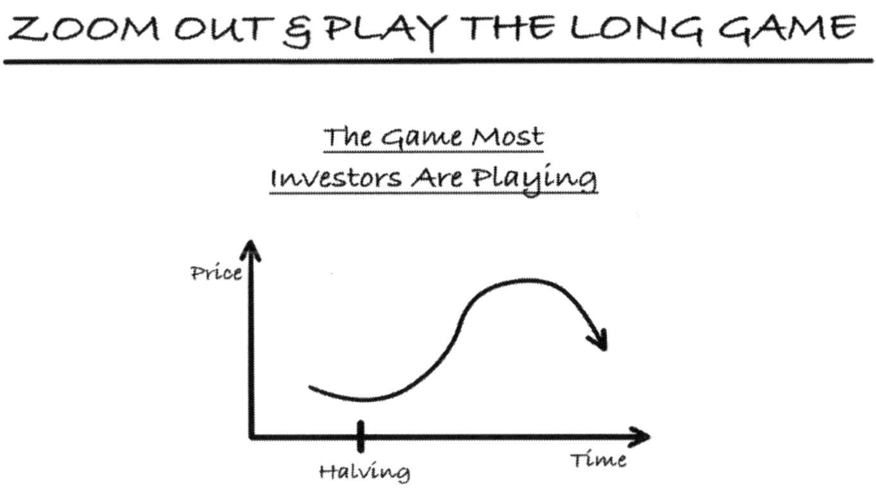

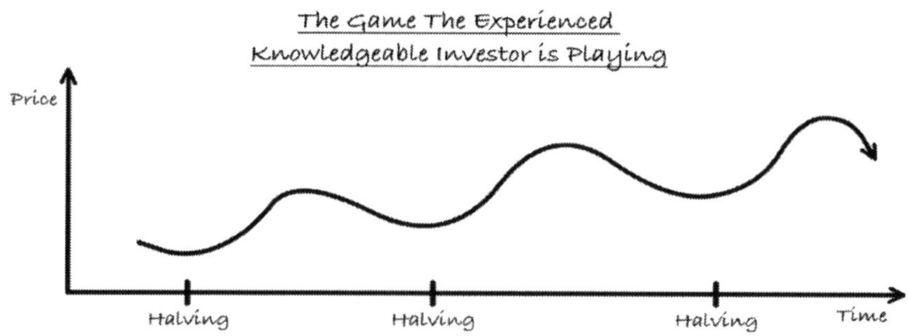

Build Real Wealth Over Multiple Four-Year Cycles

So, instead of just looking at it as one cycle, we want to look at it as multiple cycles. We have discussed holding our Bitcoin long term, but with our Altcoins, the plan is to buy, hold, sell and then repeat for the next cycle.

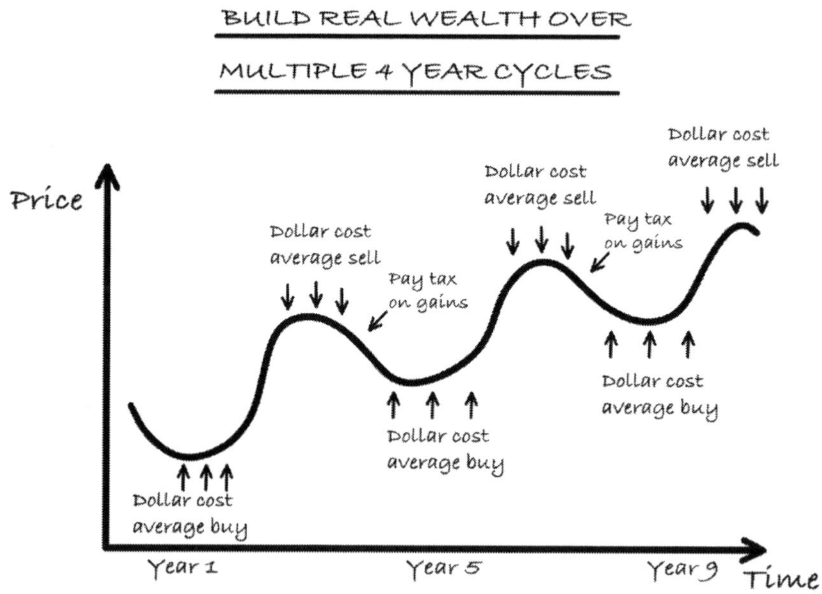

In the diagram above, we dollar-cost-average buy Altcoins in the bear market. This is followed by dollar-cost-average selling near the top of the bull market. Unfortunately, we then must pay tax on our gains, unless we are fortunate enough to live in a country that doesn't have that. Then, we repeat the cycle multiple times.

I know it's a lot to wrap your head around, but the opportunity to set yourself up for life is very worth it. The game gets exciting over time. If you think your first bull run is exciting, what about when you've taken the wins from that and then you're feeding the second one, or the third one.

Altcoin Profits & Growing the Number of Tokens

"Look for small hinges that swing big doors." – Mal Emery

We are going to cover a small hinge that swings a big door. It's a small change that can make a big difference.

The small change is buying and selling Altcoins each cycle versus holding them long term.

When I first started, I didn't realize the difference this made in terms of the number of tokens held or the profits generated.

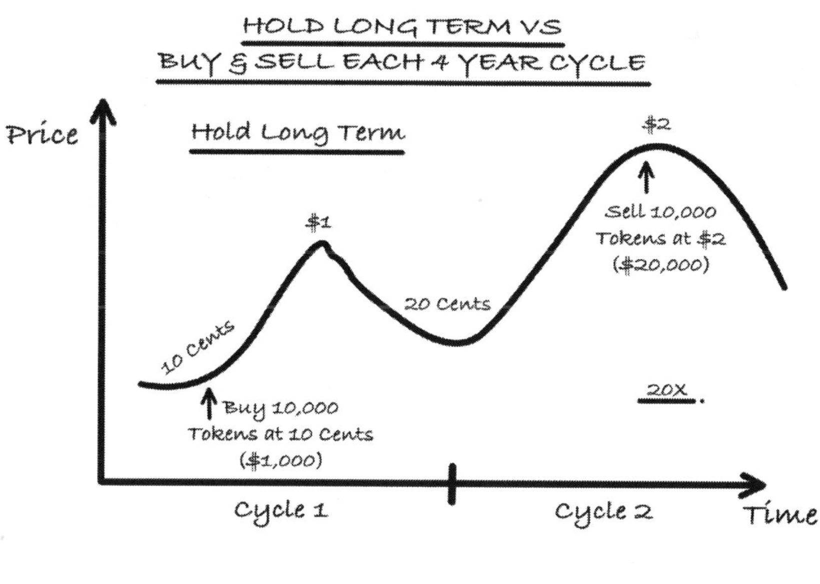

In the example above, we are holding long-term through two cycles. We buy 10,000 tokens at $0.10, and sell them at $2 each in the second cycle. This is good in that we did a 20x on our initial investment. But can we do better?

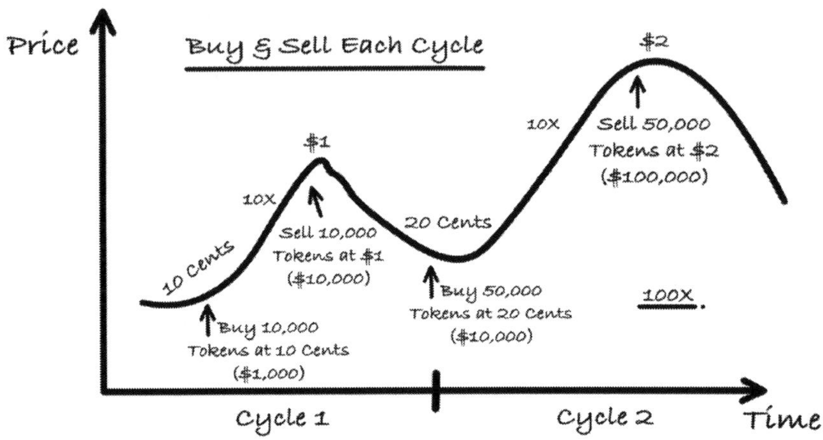

In this second example above, we buy and sell through two cycles. We buy 10,000 tokens at $0.10 and sell them at the top of the first cycle for $1.00. This gives us $10K to invest at the bottom of the next cycle. We now have enough cash to buy 50,000 tokens this time instead of the 10,000 we originally started with. Then, in the second cycle, we sell the 50,000 tokens this time and exit at $2 per token. This is outstanding because of the additional tokens we purchased in the second cycle; we now did a 100x return on our initial money invested from the beginning of the first cycle.

This is a very powerful lesson to learn. Hopefully it shows you the power of stringing multiple cycles together the optimal way.

An Example of Multiple Millions Over Multiple Cycles

For some people this will be hard to understand, especially if you are starting with small investments. If the numbers in this section don't feel comfortable, consider tens of thousands or hundreds of thousands rather than millions or multiple millions.

While the below is a hypothetical example, the numbers are quite real based on a good friend of mine, Joe, who shared with me his three-cycle journey numbers so far. This shows you what is possible when you string together multiple cycles.

TENS OF THOUSANDS TO HUNDREDS OF THOUSANDS,
HUNDREDS OF THOUSANDS TO MILLIONS,
MILLIONS TO TENS OF MILLIONS
OVER MULTIPLE CYCLES

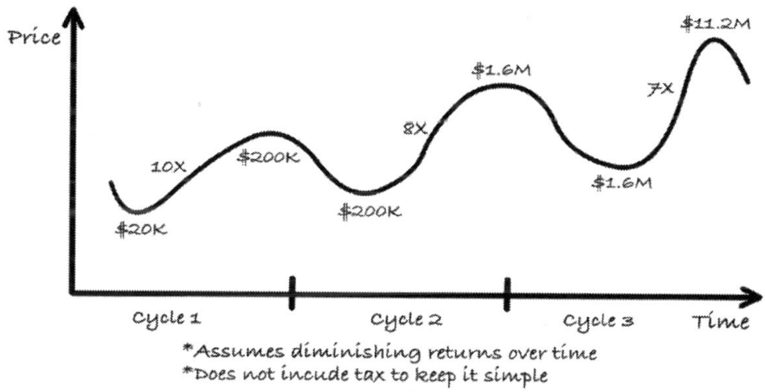

With a starting investment of $20K, by buying in the bear market and selling in the bull market, Joe was able to get a 10x on his money from the first cycle.

The $200K was then invested for an 8x return in the second cycle. The numbers are starting to get exciting now, with $1.6M exiting at the top of the second cycle.

The third cycle is playing out right now as we go to print. Based on his previous track record, we are assuming diminishing returns of 7x for Joe. This takes the third cycle investment from $1.6M to be generational wealth of roughly $11.2M by the end of the third cycle.

What About the Impact of Tax in the Same Scenario?

The example above is unrealistic in most places around the world because tax would be payable on any gains.

Every country and region will have different tax implications, but in our example below, we assumed a 20% tax to keep the math simple.

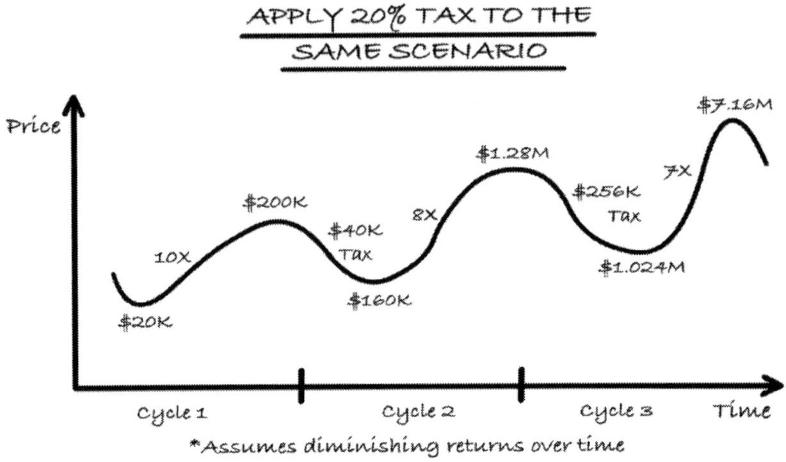

With a starting investment of $20K, Joe was able to earn 10x his money by buying in the bear market and selling in the bull market in the first cycle. Roughly $40K in tax was payable on those gains.

The $160K was then invested for an 8x in the second cycle. The numbers are impacted, but still exciting as that is $1.28m at the top of the second cycle. Roughly $256K tax was payable on those gains.

As outlined above, the third cycle is playing out as we go to print. Based on his previous track record, we are assuming diminishing returns of a 7x for Joe. This takes the third-cycle investment from $1.024M to substantial wealth of roughly $7.16M by the end of the third cycle.

You will see that taxes play a large factor in slowing down the compounding of gains. This is why many crypto investors choose to live in tax-friendly regions around the world.

Keep or Spend the Golden Goose – What is the Impact?

While the hypothetical example below is based on a close friend of mine's three-cycle journey so far, the numbers are quite real. This shows you what is possible when you string together multiple cycles.

In this context, the 'golden goose' is our capital that we have built up due to winning investments. Do we keep it to produce more golden eggs (future profits), or do we consume the golden goose for our lifestyle and expenses?

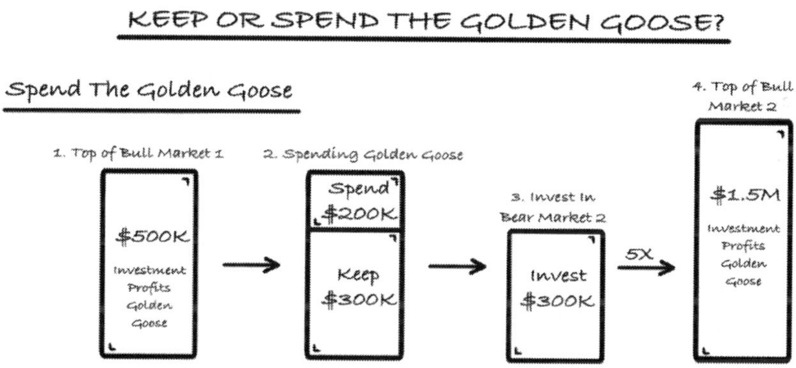

In this scenario of 'spending the golden goose,' our investor ends up with $500K after exiting at the top of bull market 1. She then spends $200K and keeps $300K to invest at the bottom of the next cycle. Assuming a 5x return, she ends up with a $1.5M 'golden goose' when exiting at the top of bull market 2.

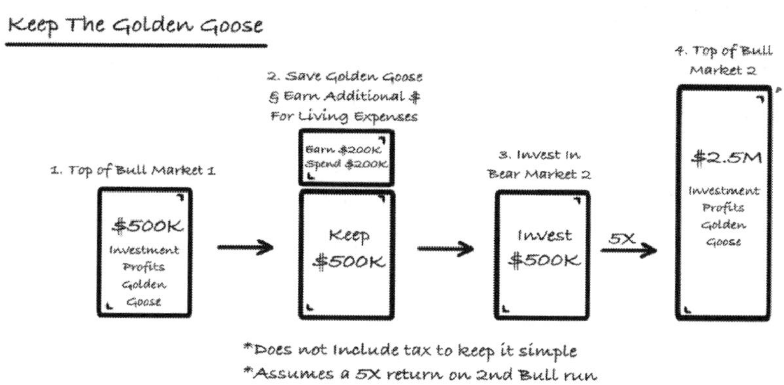

In the same scenario, but this time 'keeping the golden goose,' our investor still ends up with $500K after exiting at the top of bull market 1. She then earns $200K through work or business and spends $200K to keep the $500K to invest at the bottom of the next cycle. Assuming a 5x return, she ends up with a $2.5M golden goose when exiting at the top of bull market 2.

That is a massive $1M difference between the two scenarios, with just a single change to the input.

Keep or Spend the Golden Goose for Another Cycle – What is the Impact?

Let's build on that now. What if we added another four-year cycle to the scenario? How would that affect the numbers?

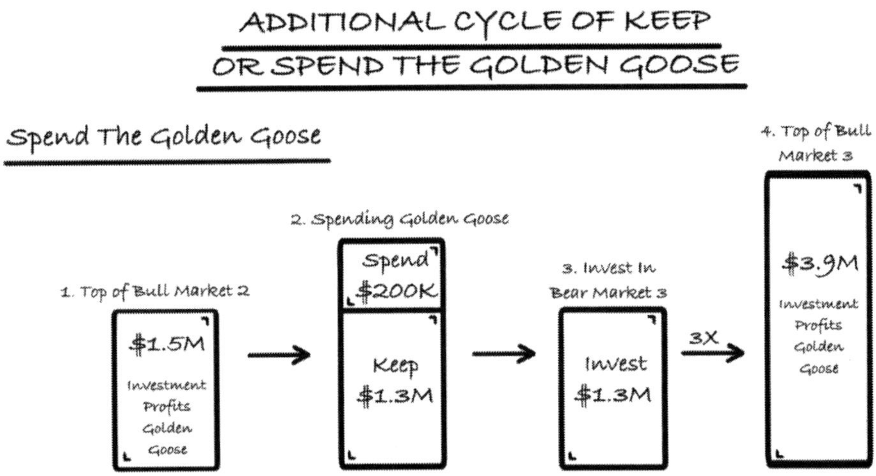

In this scenario of 'spending the golden goose,' our investor ends up with $1.5M after exiting at the top of bull market 2. She then spends $200K and keeps $1.3M to invest at the bottom of the next cycle. Assuming a 3x return, she ends up with a $3.9M golden goose when exiting at the top of bull market 3.

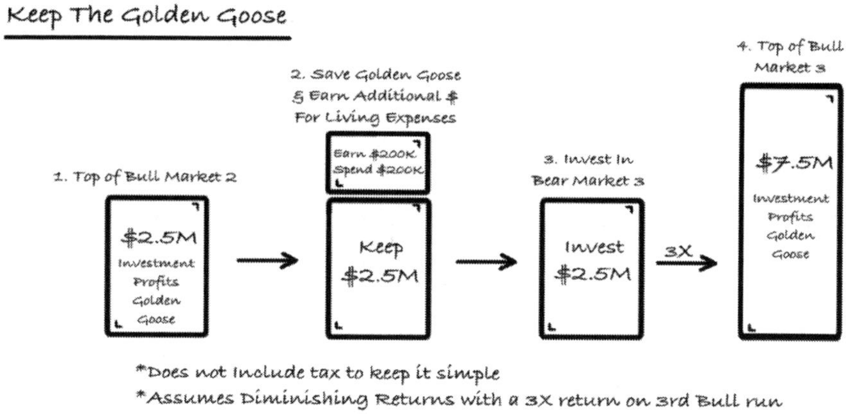

In the same scenario, but this time 'keeping the golden goose,' our investor ends up with $2.5M after exiting at the top of bull market 2. She then earns $200K through work or business and spends $200K to keep the $2.5M to invest at the bottom of the next cycle. Assuming a 3x return, she ends up with a $7.5M golden goose when exiting at the top of bull market 3.

That is a huge $3.6M difference between the two scenarios when changing whether to keep or consume the golden goose.

This exercise above really shows the power of compounding large numbers. Delaying gratification and keeping the golden goose is a smart financial decision. Additional income to cover your cost of living and expenses also has a massive impact without eroding away your golden goose capital.

But with that being said, we only live once, and there are no guarantees of tomorrow.

Personally, I am taking a balanced approach. I am re-investing most of it in future cycles to build generational wealth with my golden goose. But I'm also taking some money off the table to park in property for lifestyle and security, plus investing in fun life experiences with my family.

I don't believe there is any single 'right answer.' It's an individual decision.

Where to Park Your Cash After Exiting Your Positions

After exiting positions in profit at the top of a bull market cycle, I find the best first order of business is speaking with a qualified 'crypto-savvy' accountant about the tax liability and how to minimize that as much as possible.

Once you have put aside the money you need to give the government, it's about deciding what to do with the capital before any gets re-invested back into the bear market of the next cycle.

You have multiple options available. There is no right or wrong answer, as it's an individual choice. Please see some of the main options below.

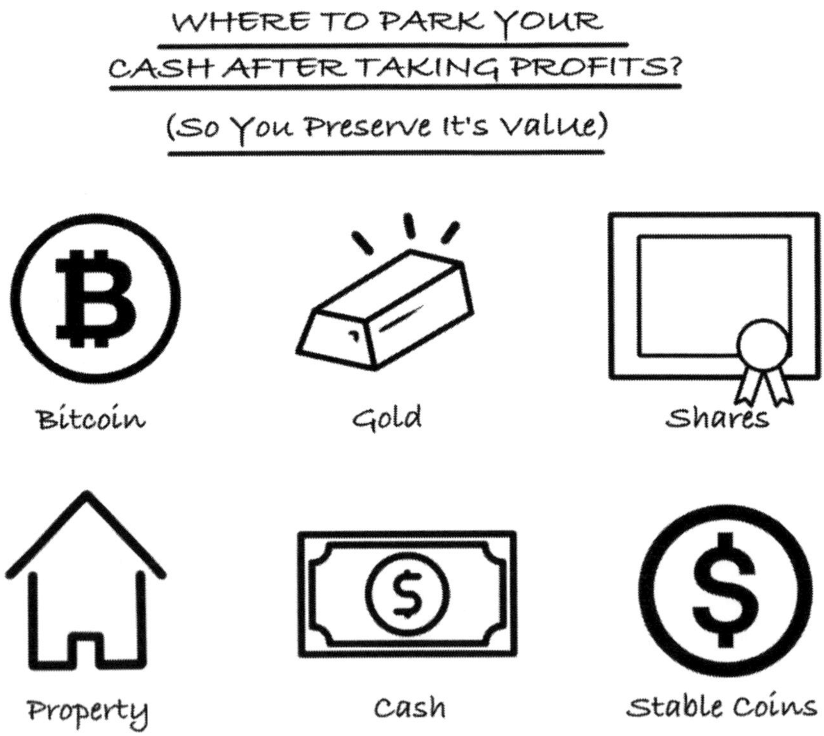

My quick thoughts on these six main options…

- Bitcoin is a very popular one. As we know, its returns have outperformed every other asset class over time. It is a scarce resource with exponential growth in demand.

- Gold historically has been a good spot to park cash. It's a scarce resource and has been going up over time, not to the same extent as Bitcoin. Still, if you want to get some capital out of crypto and diversify, gold could be a great spot.

- Shares can get steady gains over time. The risk, I think personally, is I don't like the big market corrections that can take many years to bounce back to where it was. I always ask myself, why would I put capital into shares when I can put it into crypto?

- Properties are a very good option for parking wealth. If you buy well, you can't really go too far wrong with property over time, especially if it has a land component.

- Cash feels safe, but we need to be careful. It's devaluing over time, and governments are continually printing money, causing real inflation. Out of all the options, this one is the riskiest for me personally.

- Stable coins allow you to invest in crypto quickly again, but there have been instances of stable coins failing, so they do represent a risk. Remember, a stable coin is ultimately pegged to a fiat currency, which, in my opinion, immediately makes this a risky option for long-term wealth.

- There's no right or wrong answer. We are just showing you some options, and you can go from there. The important thing is that we need to be able to access some dry powder to put into the bottom of the next cycle so that we can string together massive wealth.

Chapter 9 – Keeping Safe and Minimizing Risks with Crypto

Six Steps to Keep Safe and Minimize Your Risks With Crypto

Crypto is, without a doubt, the best financial opportunity of our lives. But it also has some bad players out to steal people's money, plus some technical risks that we need to avoid.

Let's now examine six practical steps you can take to help keep you safe and minimize the risks of investing.

1. Use a VPN Before Connecting to Exchanges

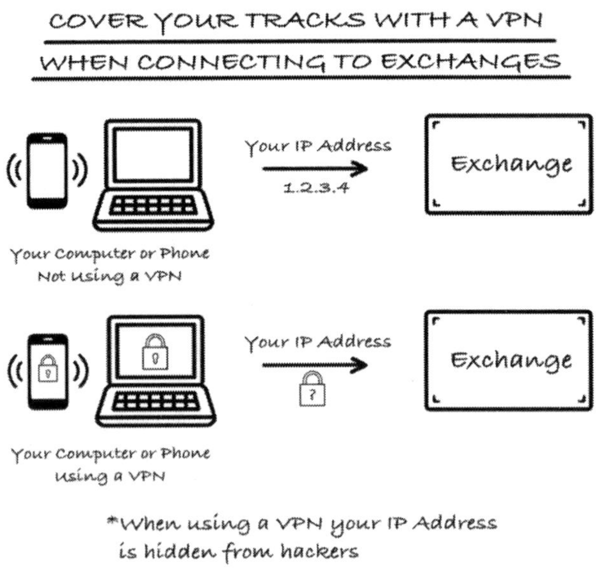

A VPN (Virtual Private Network) is a service that creates a secure, encrypted connection between your device and a remote service, such as a cryptocurrency exchange. This encrypted tunnel allows data to travel safely over the Internet, hiding your IP address and protecting your online activities from hackers.

When using a VPN, the IP address (digital identity number) of your device is hidden from hackers. This is required so that they can't learn much information about you, and they can't start to put together your whole digital footprint.

If the hackers can't really see anything about you, then you're not interesting to them. They won't build a profile on you and are less likely to try and hack you. So always, always use a VPN when connecting to cryptocurrency exchanges.

2. Minimize Your Risk with Multiple Exchanges

One is the worst number in investing. This means that we don't ever want to depend on any one important component such as one single cryptocurrency exchange.

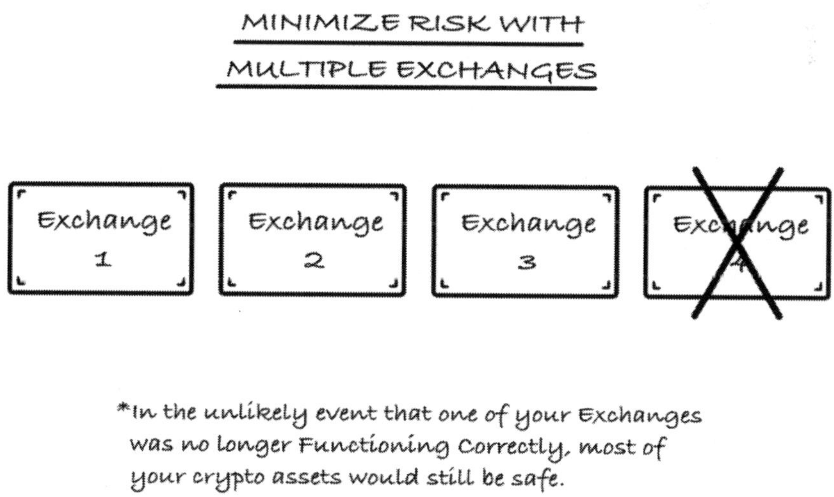

I meet many people who only want to use one exchange because that is their favorite and easy to use. I understand that, but it's taking an unnecessary risk. What happens if that exchange gets hacked? What happens if the founder of the exchange is fraudulent? What happens if the government goes after the management team of that exchange?

We don't want to have all our eggs in one basket. The easiest way to minimize this risk is with multiple exchanges. Then, if anything happened to any of them, because some value is on each exchange, in the unlikely event that one of your exchanges was no longer functioning correctly, most of your crypto assets would still be safe.

3. Hardware Wallets & Bank Vaults for Long Term Holds

Storing Crypto assets on exchanges are convenient, but it is not considered best practice. The safest approach is to store crypto assets not connected to the Internet.

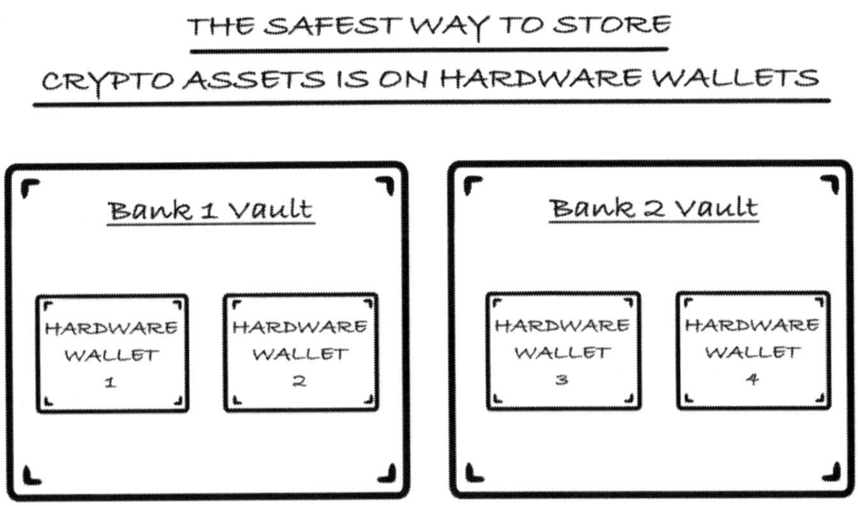

A hardware wallet is a physical device designed to securely store the private keys of cryptocurrencies offline, away from potential cyber threats.

If you buy a cryptocurrency on an exchange, you can move it off the exchange on to a hardware wallet to keep it safer.

The most common problem that I see with people's hardware wallets is they don't store them in a secure location. The hardware wallets are in places where they could get lost or stolen, like their office desk or inside their house. Putting your crypto on a hardware wallet and just leaving it at home or leaving it in your office isn't any more secure than leaving it on the exchange.

The hardware wallet should be stored in a bank vault 'safe deposit box'. This is where the bank has one key to the safe deposit box, and you have another key, and they can't access your assets. If you arc in a position where you don't feel comfortable with using a 'safe deposit box' with a bank, at the very least, don't leave your hardware wallet and private keys to your wallet in easy-to-find places like your office desk.

One is the worst number in investing, so ideally, we have multiple bank vault safe deposit boxes or multiple secure places to store your private keys to your wallet and multiple hardware wallets with our crypto assets spread across them.

4. Password Management Software and Two-Factor Authentication

The way most people do security access is not good enough for crypto. Common security mistakes I see in this area include:

- Writing down your password, and sticking it on your monitor.
- Writing your passwords in a book that's in an easy-to-find location at home.
- Saving your passwords in a spreadsheet or document that's on your computer.
- Using the same password across all your systems.

- The password is easy-to-remember, simple words and numbers.
- Relying on passwords alone (not two-factor authentication).

Are you guilty of any of these? Don't worry, you are not alone. But if you are going to build wealth in cryptocurrency, you need to be more secure than that, so you don't risk losing it to hackers.

The best way to do this is a two-pronged approach.

The first step is to create long, complex, unique passwords, which are a combination of random letters, numbers, and special characters. These will be impossible to remember. That's okay; we use password management software with a strong password and two-factor authentication to access it.

The second step is to enable two-factor authentication on all your systems, such as exchanges, that you access. Two-factor authentication (2FA) is a security process in which you provide two different authentication factors to verify your identity. This method enhances the security of online accounts by requiring something you know (like a password) and also something you have (like a mobile device).

The most common 2FA service is Google Authenticator, which is an App that runs on your phone and provides a unique random rotating number. Once enabled, you would require a password and your 2FA code from your phone to access a crypto exchange. This means if a hacker gets your password, they still can't log in to steal your crypto assets unless they also have access to your phone and it's unlocked.

5. Anti-Virus and Phishing Suite

The next step is to avoid malware, viruses and phishing attacks.

Malware is malicious software that has been written and deployed in such a way that someone is trying to steal your information or compromise/sell your data.

A virus is a type of malware that is designed to spread from device to device, causing harm or stealing data.

Phishing attacks are where hackers try to get you to share personal information. You might receive an email, an SMS or a link that is malicious. Often the hackers want you to connect to something, or they want you to share your username and password or some personal information about yourself so that they can log into your account and steal your crypto.

We need to avoid all of these. Essentially, we need to run a comprehensive antivirus and anti-phishing suite software package designed to identify and stop these threats.

You shouldn't just use a free one, either. It should be a paid service because a paid one will get updated more often. A free service will likely be out of date and only get updated periodically.

Ultimately, no random person will ever reach out to you via email, SMS, social media or anything else and offer you 'free' crypto or any other amazing offer they may send. If it sounds too good to be true, it's most likely exactly that. Not true.

6. Safely Move Crypto Assets Between Wallets

As discussed previously, it's best practice to have multiple hardware wallets and/or multiple exchanges (an online wallet). So, if we have all our crypto assets on one wallet, how do we safely transfer them to another wallet?

THE SAFE WAY TO MOVE CRYPTO ASSETS BETWEEN WALLETS

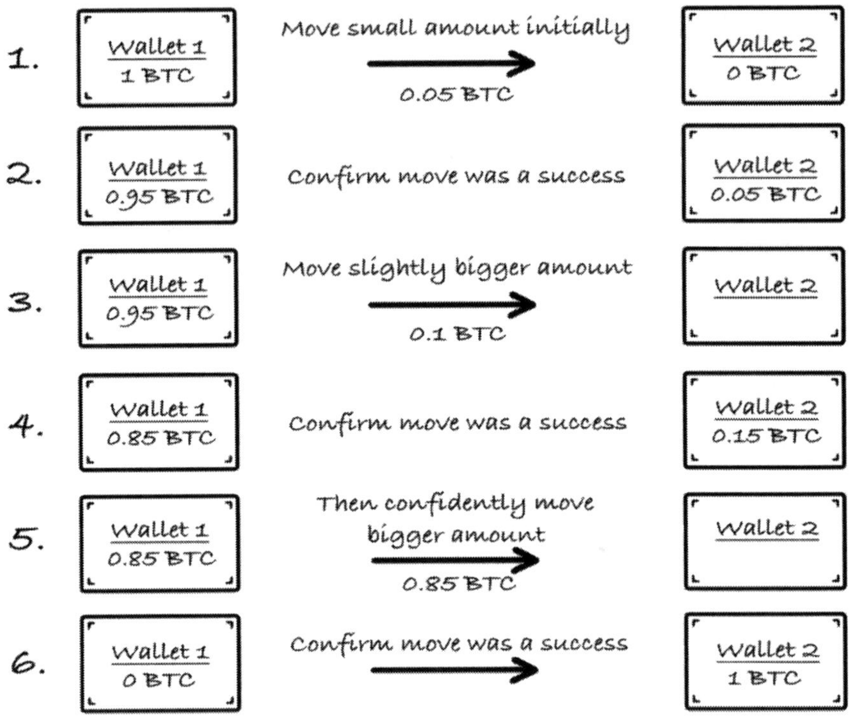

*This is an example of how to safely move Bitcoin (BTC) between Exchanges or Hardware Wallets.

The example above shows how to move Bitcoin between exchanges or hardware wallets safely. The technique is to do it slowly and carefully in bite sized chunks.

If you wanted to move a whole Bitcoin, you wouldn't just copy a whole Bitcoin across from one wallet to another. In my opinion, you would move across part of a Bitcoin and verify that it was received before you move more or larger values.

As the old saying goes, it’s better off to be safe than sorry.

PART 2 – WHO YOU NEED TO BECOME TO BE AT THE RIGHT LEVEL TO JOIN THE CRYPTO NEW RICH

Chapter 10 – Vision & Goals For Achieving Success

Who Do I Need to Become?

"Most people want to change their circumstances to improve their lives, instead of changing themselves to improve their circumstances." – John C Maxwell

We discussed early on that joining the Crypto New Rich is a learnable skill. Hopefully, I have now delivered on my promise of showing you *'What you need to know about crypto to join the new rich.'*

I have this saying: "*You bring yourself to the deal,*" so you need to show up as the very best version of yourself with your investing. That is why we will now transition into focussing on the most important part, which is *'Who do you need to become to be at the right level to join the Crypto New Rich?'*

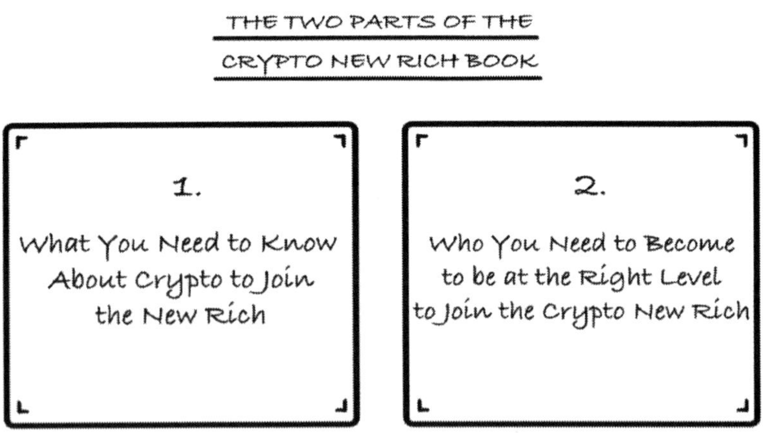

Life doesn't actually get easier. You just get stronger, more educated, and more knowledgeable and develop a better mindset and emotional intelligence. Effectively, over time, you bring a better version of yourself to the deal.

A better question than *'What do I need to learn?'* is *'Who do I need to become?'* to achieve that next level of success.

That is very smart. It's like basically saying what happens if you get to the end of your life and then you meet the other version of you? One guy/girl has sat on the couch the whole time, and then the other guy/girl has gone on and had an amazing impact on the world. The same person, but two completely different paths....

A Fog Over the Land For 97%

"We have two lives and the second begins when we realize we only have one." – Confucius

How many people do you know who complain about their job, the traffic, their life, and everything else – but they never take any action to do anything about it? It's like there's a fog over the land for 97% of people. They're not really going to do anything about it.

In the movie *Braveheart*, the character William Wallace talks wisely about freedom as he says, *"Every man dies, but not every man really lives."*

When I heard that it really made me think, especially as we get older, we really, really need to focus on living.

We can't be the complainers and the non-action takers. You and I are different – we are going to do something about it and change our lives to be more abundant, have more options and be more fun.

Can't Worry About What Others Will Think

I noticed that people laughed at me all along on my investing journey. *"How's your magical internet money going? Are you rich yet?"* and all this kind of stuff.

But these days, with the freedom and abundance I have created in my life by implementing exactly what I have been teaching you here. Those folks are not really laughing at me so much anymore.

I think I used to be a little bit paralyzed by fear of worrying about what these people thought about me if I made a mistake. It doesn't matter what they think because those people who were laughing at me along the way are now asking, *"Could you help me to do that?"*

The Mind, A Heat Seeking Missile

Your subconscious mind deals in 'exacts' just like a heat-seeking missile. If your goal is non-specific, like *'I want to make more money'* after you have some wins with your investing, your brain thinks, *"Did we make more money? Yes. We can turn off."*

A heat-seeking missile works by saying, *"Hey, did we hit a heat source? Yes, but it is not big enough – keep going."* Your subconscious brain works exactly the same way.

Whereas, if instead we have a specific goal of *'we want to hit this $250K in profit this market cycle'*, then the subconscious brain says, *"Did we hit it? No. Keep scrambling. Did we hit it? No. Keep scrambling"*, and so on until you reach that specific goal.

For the subconscious brain, goals need to be meaningful, specific, and ultimately documented.

What Does Success Mean to You?

What are you chasing or building? For me, it's really about freedom, provision and security.

Freedom: I want and have built with crypto the freedom to live where I want to live, to work when I want to work (but not be a wage slave), to have quality family time, to hang out with only positive, like-minded people and to travel and see the world.

Provision: Success is also about providing for my family and loved ones. I don't want to spoil my kids by giving them everything, but I also don't want them to have to go without essentials like good food, healthcare and education.

Security: By building a big golden goose and continuing to stack SATs, I've been able to create security and certainty in my family's financial future so that we won't have to be stressed in retirement.

Your Purpose and Reason Why

"Everybody has a calling and your real job in life is to figure out as soon as possible what that is, who you were meant to be and to begin to honor that in the best way possible for yourself." – Oprah Winfrey

The quality of the question determines the quality of the answer, and an even more powerful question than one about goals is, 'What is my purpose?'

When we first start on our journey, it is often about us – about getting out of debt, getting ahead in life, having a good car, a good house and some money in the bank.

Then, the next stage often involves spoiling ourselves with nice toys and fun experiences.

Ultimately, our goals, if we want to design and have happiness in the long term, need to be about more than just us. Growth and contribution give us fulfillment, meaning and happiness.

A good exercise is to stop and think: *What was I put on this earth to do? If money wasn't an issue, what would I be doing? What would I be working on? What is my purpose? What am I so passionate about that it would be fun/interesting/fulfilling to work on even if I wasn't getting paid or any recognition?*

The great thing about this is the more we grow, the more we can contribute and give. Mal Emery says, *"As a poor man or woman, there is very little impact you can have on the world due to lack of leverage, but as a rich man or woman..."*

What can you do to create a positive ripple effect in the world over time? What is to be your contribution greater than yourself?

E.S.E

Ultimately, if we are going to implement our vision and reach our goals and purpose, we need E.S.E., which is a simple formula for highly effective investing, business and life. We need a combination of all three.

E – Education and Knowledge

S – Strategy

E – Execution

Education and Knowledge: Most people stop their education process when they finish high school or university. They basically switch off and think that they are done with it. The way I look at it is that you just finished the first quarter of the game, and there is a lot left to be played. *"You are what you know,"* so be a continual lifelong student. I look at myself as an intellectual athlete. Being a crypto-nerd these days is cool, as there is good money in it.

Strategy: Most people love the *'tactics'* of the next hack or shortcut that will give them an advantage rather than the big-picture business *'strategy,'* which makes the difference. You have to think about investing like a General. It doesn't matter if you lose an individual battle (investment), if you have a strategy (like multiple cycles) and are playing the long game to win the overall war.

Execution: This last one can be the difference between success and failure. Success follows speed. You can learn the best investment strategies and tactics in the world, but if you do nothing with them, you will get zero results. If you have done your research, you are confident in a project, and the timing is right for an entry, then you need to go for it.

E.S.E

3 Essential Components For Reaching Our Goals

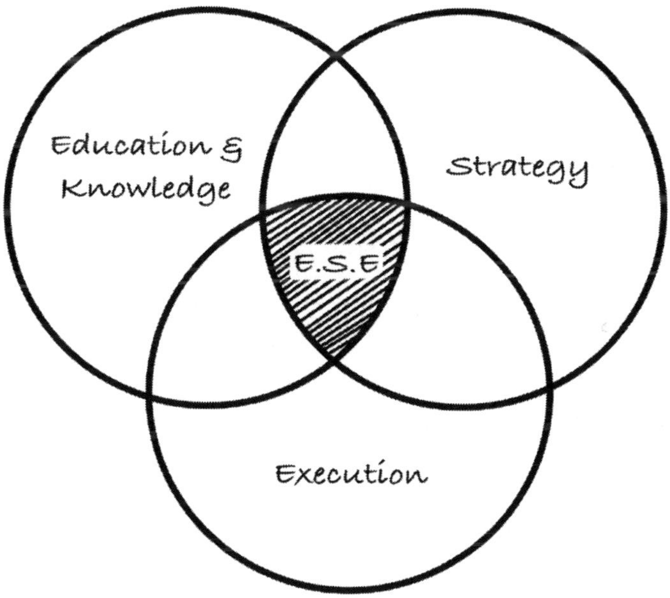

What Exactly Do You Want to Achieve from Your Investing?

Now, we need to transition to be more specific about goals with our investing. You now need to have an answer to the question of *'what exactly do you want to achieve from your investing – both short term and long term?'*

What are you trying to get? Are you trying to buy a new house? Upgrade your house? Get the capital to start a new business so that you have more dry powder coming in to feed the beast? Get out of your day job? Buy your dream car? Plus, in reality, you should also be after golden goose profits to set you up for the next cycle?

Those are just a few examples, but you need to really know and write down what you want to achieve. Be meaningful and specific about what you want from your investing.

How Many Cycles Will It Take to Achieve It?

My short-term cycle goals have been improving my standard of living, having amazing experiences with the family and increasing my security by having more cash available reserves.

In the longer term, I've been working towards having 100 Bitcoins safely held in my hardware wallet. With that achievement, life feels very safe and has great options regarding where I live, how I live, where I travel, and the work and life choices I can make from there. I'd love to say that I achieved that in my first two cycles, but the reality is that I didn't. But I'm well on track to achieving it by the end of my third or fourth cycle.

Do you have a net worth number with your longer-term goals, like the amount in my example above? What do you think is realistic on how many cycles you need to string together to achieve it? When hitting a longer-term number goal, remember that the more you buy in the bear, not in the top of the bull, as well as feed the beast and reinvest the golden goose, the faster you will get there.

What Specific Amount Do You Want to Achieve This Cycle?

Do you have a specific number in mind that you are trying to hit at the peak of the bull market in your current cycle?

It will be different for everyone. Yours could be $10K, $100K, $1M, $10M, or whatever.

Also give thought to what tax are you going to have to pay on those gains, as that is going to affect it.

What are you planning on spending? What golden goose capital will you have to invest in the next cycle?

With Your Allocated Capital What Multiple Do You Need to Achieve?

Do you need to earn 5x on your money this cycle to achieve your goals, e.g., turn $10K into $50K? If so, that may be realistic, depending on when you bought and how good your portfolio allocation is.

If you bought it towards the bottom and then you're timing it well to sell out near the top, then sometimes as high as 10x on your money or more may be achievable. If you're shooting for 20x and more on your money through this cycle, you may be unrealistic.

Who knows? You may achieve it, but not many people are 20x their money in a cycle. Everyone's individual results will vary. If you think about it, even making your money grow 10% or 20% in a year is pretty exciting in normal investing outside of crypto.

Sometimes, we won't hit our goal this cycle, and that's OK. I've seen investors holding on to achieve their desired multiples on their portfolios, but they ignored or didn't understand the market cycle. They rode the market up and held on to their Altcoins too long, only to ride it back down to much lower prices.

That's why taking profits as we go is always important, especially towards the top half of the bull market. This is like the proverb *'a bird in the hand is worth two in the bush.'*

Chapter 11 – Emotional Intelligence For Success

Quality of Investing, Life and Emotions

Many people talk about the 'millionaire mindset,' but don't focus enough on their emotions.

Warren Buffett wisely says, *"Until you manage your emotions, don't expect to manage your money."* From my experience, this is 100% true. Here are two investors – Investor A can control her emotions. Investor B gets upset and panics every time the market does a correction. Which of these investors do you believe will be more successful over time?

It's safe to say that your emotions will affect your investing, but what about other areas of your life?

Tony Robbins advises, *"The quality of your life is not what is happening to you; it's the quality of your emotions."*

Your emotions can have a massive impact on your life because they affect the quality of your day, your decisions and even the quality of the day of those around you.

When I first started on this journey as an entrepreneur and investor, I was naïve and had no idea 'emotions' was an area that was even important or relevant. I learned over time that it is equally as important as your millionaire mindset.

I always live by the mantra, *'work harder on yourself than you do on your business and investing.'* This is based on something that really hit me when I discovered it. It's from Jim Rohn: *"Income seldom exceeds personal development."*

This is such an important chapter because we can implement all the things that we covered together in Part 1 on crypto, but if we don't have good emotional intelligence and a strong millionaire mindset, we can sabotage it all.

A catamaran is a multi-hulled watercraft with two parallel hulls of equal size. The twin-hull design provides stability and speed. Some of the things in this chapter could be considered a millionaire mindset, and some of the things in the next chapter could be considered emotional intelligence. They are very closely related, and like the catamaran's hulls, we need both of them to be successful.

Emotional Intelligence Definition

Emotional intelligence (EI or EQ) has two parts: the ability to recognize, understand and manage our emotions and the ability to recognize, understand and influence the emotions of others.

The scope of this journey we are on together is about our self-improvement and setting ourselves up for life with investing. While the second part about 'emotional intelligence with others' is important, it is beyond the scope of what we will cover together. I strongly recommend you go deep on the subject, as it's a game changer.

Operating System & Freedom From

I've never met Naval Ravikant personally, but he, like Tony Robbins, has been one of my most impactful coaches, especially in the inner game. If you haven't read *The Almanack of Naval Ravikant*, I strongly recommend you do so, as it's jam-packed full of wisdom. I can't recommend it highly enough.

To quote Naval, *"I really value freedom, but it's now a different definition of freedom. My old definition was 'freedom to.' Freedom to do anything I want. Freedom to do whatever I feel like, whenever I feel like. Now the freedom I'm looking for is internal freedom. It's 'freedom from.' Freedom from reaction, freedom from feeling angry, freedom from being sad, freedom from being forced to do things."*

This is very wise and was a massive learning experience for me. I have worked on my emotional intelligence to get to the point where I try to control my emotions. The idea is to get to the point where external factors do not sway me.

This builds into the concept that your emotional intelligence and mindset are like an operating system. It is the underlying program that runs everything you do, experience and feel.

In this model, your body is like hardware, and all the specialized skills you learn are like software that runs on top of the operating system. See the diagram below.

YOUR HARDWARE, OPERATING SYSTEM & SOFTWARE

Software	Your Specialized Skills
Operating System	Your Mindset & Emotions
Hardware	Your Body

Roly Poly Doll Operating System Upgrade

A Roly Poly doll, also known as a tilting doll, is a traditional toy with a rounded, weighted base that allows it to return to an upright position after being tilted to one side. This type of doll is designed to wobble and sway back and forth when pushed, but it always stands back up due to its low center of gravity.

With my emotional intelligence operating system, I try to always be like the Roly Poly doll. This means trying to have happy, steady, calm emotions all the time, or most of the time, but ideally all the time. Think of this as our Roly Poly doll standing upright.

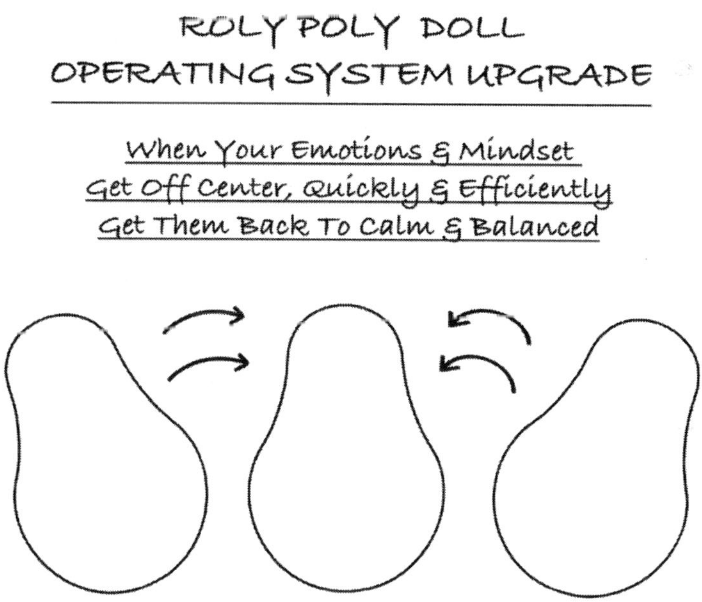

When something happens that upsets me in any way, I think of this as my Roly Poly doll operating system being on an angle/tilt. I don't let it keep me out of tilt. I try to get back to steady, calm, and zen with my Roly Poly doll operating system, which is upright again, as quickly as possible. Give this focused, emotional awareness strategy a try. It's what many of the most successful people in the world do.

Eight Things We Can Focus on To Improve Emotional Intelligence for Our Investing Journey

Let's focus on eight specific ways to improve our emotional intelligence to make our investing journey more successful.

1. Remove All Emotion from Our Investing

When investing, we want 'logic' not 'emotion.' The best decisions are rarely made when we are highly emotional. The higher the emotion, the lower the quality of the decisions.

"What's going on with Bitcoin? Why is it going down? This isn't supposed to be happening." Ever heard any of your friends or acquaintances say things like that in an agitated state? I know I certainly have. It's always from someone new to investing or someone who can't manage their emotions.

If you run your emotions like that, unfortunately, you're not likely to be successful in this investing game, unless you can control them and fix them.

2. Identify, Be Aware and Catch Our Emotions

It's normal and perfectly fine to experience emotions that don't support or help us. We just don't want to leave them 'un-checked.'

We need to be an external observer of our emotions and identify/catch them when our Roly Poly doll is on a tilt and identify: *"Is this helping me, or is it hurting me?"* If the emotion is not serving you well, do whatever it takes, such as changing your physical state, controlling deep breathing and talking to yourself to get your operating system back to steady, calm and zen as quickly as possible. The more zen-like we are, the more successful we will be with investing.

3. *Self-Regulation – Pause, Calm Before React*

We can't avoid bad stuff from happening to us. It's not about if it's going to happen; it's more about when it is going to happen.

When that does happen, an important part of emotional intelligence is taking time to pause, gather our thoughts, stop and breathe. We want to be calm so that we can think before we react.

Slowing things down and building in a little time buffer is a great way of avoiding bad decisions made in times of heated emotions.

Someone very smart once said to me, *"Troy, never send an email or text message when you're angry or upset. Always keep that message in your drafts and wait until the next day."* I've lived by this statement with my written communication, and let me tell you, I have never once sent one of those messages sitting in my drafts the next day.

4. *Control Our Emotional Intelligence Waves*

I have found that the most successful entrepreneurs and investors, as a general rule, have good emotional intelligence waves.

They can control their emotions much more smoothly and evenly than unsuccessful entrepreneurs and investors, who tend to *'flip out'* more and go from happy to upset rather than happy to calm.

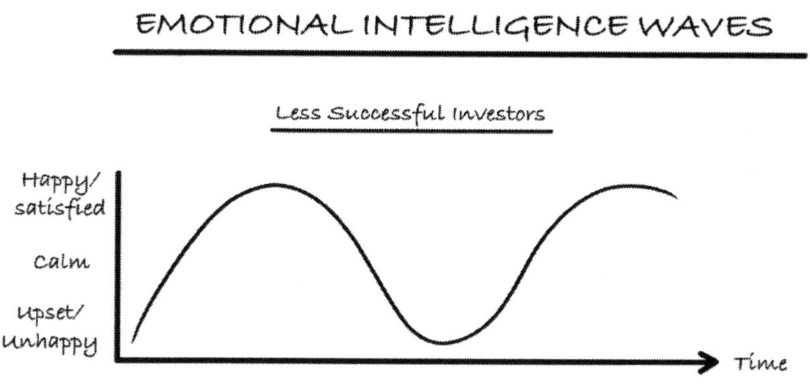

In the example above, the less successful investor regularly experiences large emotional swings from happy to unhappy. The more successful investor in the example below controls his emotions to flow from happy to calm while avoiding the upset/unhappy.

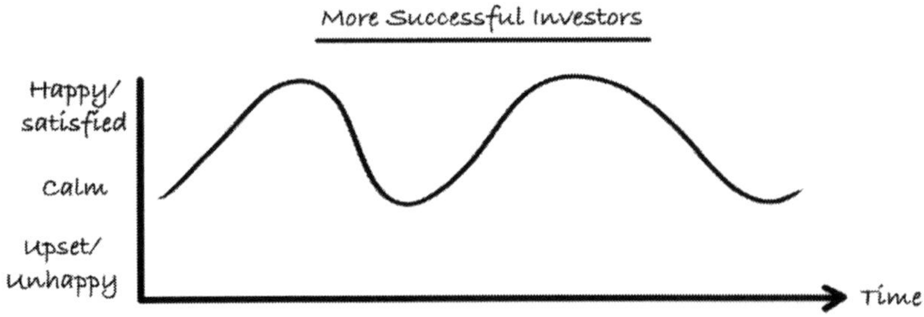

If you're constantly up and then down, the quality of your life and the decisions you make will not be that great.

5. Apply Logic & Avoid FOMO in Bull Market Conditions

Have you ever experienced FOMO (fear of missing out) when investing, or is it just me?

In bull market conditions, it's very common to develop opinion bias, where we focus on the opinions of others that align with our own. The triangulation technique, which compares multiple experts' market analyses, combined with our knowledge of the previous cycles and current technical analysis, can help us avoid making emotional mistakes.

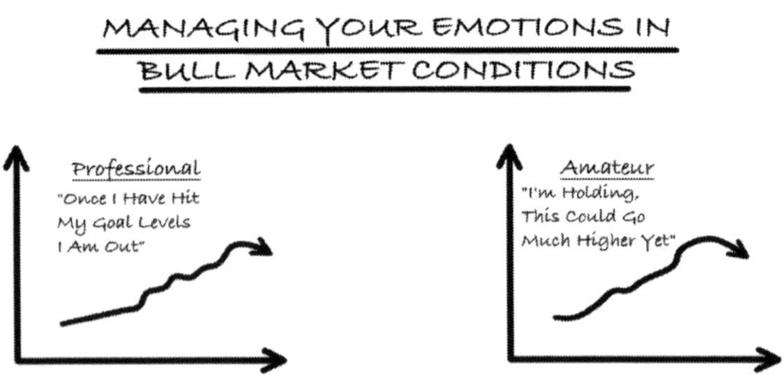

In upward-trending markets, there is always the thought, *"If I sell now, I could miss all the future gains."* While that is true, it's important to think more like the professional investor in our example above, who has a strategy and goal levels that they're working towards. Once they hit their goal level, they exit the market.

The amateur holds on to his positions, thinking, *"This is going to keep going, this is going much higher."* They never dollar cost average exit near the top. They end up in a situation where the market turns, and then there are not enough buyers. There are more sellers than buyers, so they can't necessarily get out of their positions.

We need to be okay with maybe missing the top 10% of the market price appreciation. It doesn't matter if we rode it all the rest of the way up. If we got out with cash, we would have good funds available to invest at the bottom of the next bear cycle.

6. *Zoom Out and Avoid Emotions Causing Realised Losses in Market Corrections*

On the flip side, how do we manage our emotions in downward-trending markets? We need to zoom out and avoid emotions that cause realized losses in market corrections.

The first step is to zoom out for perspective. In the example below, you can see that the investor is looking at only the current timeframe market data and is stressed about a market correction.

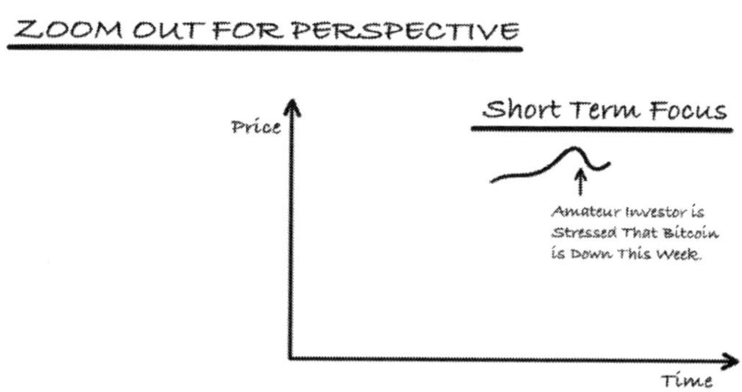

The professional investor controls their emotions and, on the charts, zooms out to see the context of the current market correction. In the example below, we can see when zoomed out that the current market downturn is likely just a normal market correction on an overall positive market trajectory. The market's going along, it corrects downwards, and then it's potentially going back up again. This is all completely normal when you zoom out and view the long-term market structure.

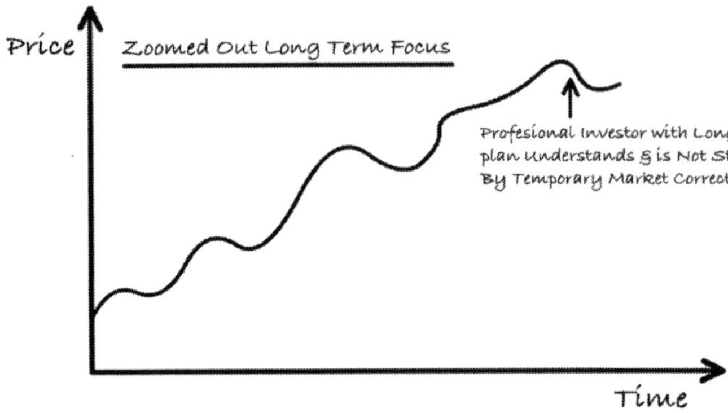

Only when we sell do we lose the gains and realize any losses.

See the example below. The professional investor makes an analyzes that it's just a market correction, controls their emotions and sticks with their Crypto Pentagon strategy/gameplan.

The amateur, on the other hand, is stressed. They can't handle the stress and are exiting the market in losing positions. That's not the path to joining the Crypto New Rich.

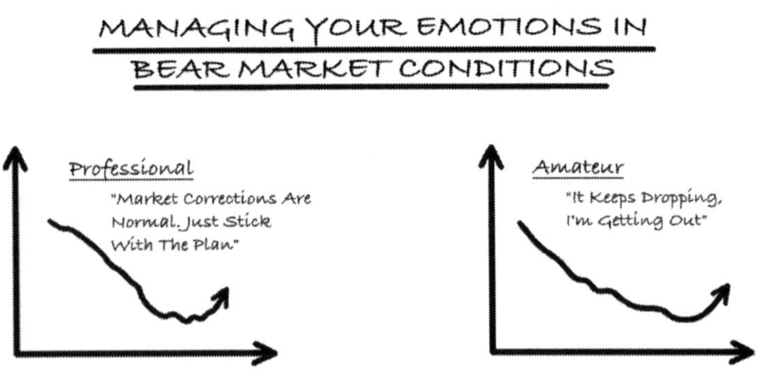

Calm, logic, knowledge, and market analysis are very important here. Sometimes, we may really feel or identify that this is the top of the market cycle. We feel that exiting the market to avoid further losses may be the best course of action. Most elite football players have a game plan, and they stick to it. The average football player doesn't have a plan. They will play the game that is in front of them at the time.

We are no different, except the average crypto investor doesn't have the same physical skills as the football player (although usually a much better bank balance). We need to always display the elite football player mentality. Have your game plan and stick to it. Don't be taken off track by the market that is in front of you at the time.

7. *Take Ownership of All Decisions & Avoid the Blame Game*

"I was served lemons, but I made lemonade." – Hattie White, American educator and politician

A lesson I learned along the journey was to take ownership of my decisions and avoid the blame game.

If I entered or exited the market at the wrong time, I'm 100% responsible, as I must have missed some key analysis or lessons. If I bought into a project that ended up upside down, there is no one else to blame but me. I'm 100% responsible, as I must have misjudged the project.

We can reduce future mistakes by doing a quick analysis of *"What can I take from that so that I learn and make better decisions moving forward?"*

We are playing an exponential investing game, and the ups are far bigger than the downs. If you play the blame game, you're never going to win. The good thing is you always get another swing at bat, as there will be more market cycles just around the corner.

As investors, we need to manage our emotions calmly, using the mantra, *"I'm the captain of this ship. All the decisions, both good and bad, are mine. I'm just going to wear it. I'm going to learn from it, and we're going to move on."*

8. Master Fear & Don't Let it Hold You Back from Decisions & Action

"The primary difference between rich people and poor people is how they handle fear." – Robert Kiyosaki

When we are born, we have only two innate fears: the fear of falling and the fear of loud sounds. Let's think about all the other fears we have developed over time. They have been learned through observation of what is happening around us and observing and modeling the social behaviors of others.

Fear is the biggest thing that holds people back. Related to that is *"What will people say about me if I get it wrong?"*

But what will they say about you if you get it right? If you get this right, you win the prize of freedom and living life on your terms.

You can't worry about what other people think about you. You've got to master your fear and be in control of it. Be calm, make good decisions, move quickly, and take massive action.

"The biggest reason why so many people are unhappy right now is because they value someone else's opinion more than their own. Once you get past that, life can get real good." – Gary Vaynerchuk, American businessman, author, speaker and Internet personality

Let's now move on to the second related hull: our millionaire mindset.

CHAPTER 12 – MILLIONAIRE MINDSET

Bringing Yourself to the Deal

"You can't build a million-dollar business with a two-dollar mindset."
– Pat Mesiti, Australian entrepreneur and speaker

Similarly, you can't build a million-dollar portfolio without developing and enhancing your mindset.

That quote above from Pat is 100% correct. In the past, I've seen amazing business and investment opportunities that ticked all the right boxes, but they didn't work the way they should. Generally, the reason is that the investor/entrepreneur brought themselves to the deal.

That means their mindset was restricting them in such a way that it wasn't conducive to success. They were sabotaging themselves, most often subconsciously, not even realizing that they were doing it.

Millionaires think, act and behave differently from most people. They even control their emotions differently from average people.

This success mindset area is perhaps the most important of everything we will cover together. Without it firing optimally, your investing success can all come to nothing.

Tony Robbins believes success is as much as 80% mindset. He is famous for saying, *"I've found it's 80 percent psychology and 20 percent skills."*

Your Best Investment is in You

"Become a millionaire not for the million dollars, but for what it will make of you to achieve it." – Jim Rohn

I am often asked about investing and where people should invest their money. My reply is always the same: *"You, your knowledge and your mindset are your greatest asset because you are what you know, so invest your money first in your learning."*

I find developing a mindset *'a journey'* rather than *'a destination.'* It's a lifelong pursuit of mastery. I don't hear many successful people saying, *'I'm not wasting my time and money on that success mindset crap.'*

This really hit me when I learned this from Jim Rohn: *"Income seldom exceeds personal development."*

Your most important investment isn't in Bitcoin or Altcoin; it's in yourself: your mindset, knowledge, and emotional intelligence. You are the one variable that will remain constant throughout your lifetime investing journey.

If you haven't already done so, I recommend you invest in yourself and grab the video training that accompanies this book. They are designed to work together.

SPECIAL OFFER TO GIVE YOU AN UNFAIR ADVANTAGE

Get the Crypto New Rich Video Training Course That Compliments This Book

Includes

- ✓ What You Need to Know About Crypto to Join the New Rich
- ✓ Who You Need to Become to be at the Right Level to Join the Crypto New Rich

Invest in Your Education to Fast Track Your Crypto Journey

See CryptoNewRich.com/course

The Right Spot at the Right Time?

"I know the mind, like the parachute, is most valuable open." – Dan Kennedy, American marketing expert and public speaker

Up until a certain age, I thought, *"You have to be in the right spot, at the right time."* I believed that's how you get lucky.

But I didn't realize that the reality was that you had to be in the right spot with the right mindset. I later figured out the correct version, which is, *"You have to be the right person, with the right mindset, in the right spot at the right time."*

How many people have you talked to about Bitcoin and crypto? How many have listened to you? Not many, right? Those people all have the same life-changing opportunity as you and I do right now, but they are not yet the right person with the right mindset in the right spot at the right time.

If You Want a Different Result

"The winners in life think constantly in terms of I can, I will, and I am. Losers, on the other hand, concentrate their waking thoughts on what they should have or would have done, or what they can't do." – Dennis Waitley, American motivational speaker, writer and consultant

If you want a different result from everyone else, you can't do the same as the masses.

It will do us no good to complain that *'life isn't fair,'* but that is very common to hear from people.

Instead, we need a different winning mindset of *'I'll do whatever it takes.'* This means that we need to focus on how we can keep learning, evolving and growing to the point where we earn, deserve and get the wealth.

Let's now look at 12 mindset essentials for engineering the success you desire, which can lead to creating your dream lifestyle and, ultimately, freedom.

Twelve Mindset Essentials for Extraordinary Success, Lifestyle and Freedom

1. Focus

Number one is focus. If you're scattered and learning eight different investment strategies, your chances success in any of them are meager.

There is a saying: *"He/she who chases two rabbits catches none,"* as they both run off in different directions, and we can't be in two spots at the same time.

I meet investors who tell me they are *'Doing a bit of buy-and-hold crypto, plus day trading shares, renovating and flipping properties, and learning the collectible watch business.'* That may be an extreme example, but you get the idea. To that investor, I say, *'Stop, choose one and cull the rest. Once you have mastered it, if you want to, you can look at other investment strategies, but not before then.'*

Sometimes, as humans, we get bored of doing just one thing and see the next bright, shiny object and chase it, thinking it's going to be better rather than sticking with what's working.

We get what we focus on. This means that focusing solely on mastering one investment strategy gives us the greatest chance of success.

2. Patience

Be willing to play the long game to win. Everyone wants to get rich overnight but remember what we covered in our section on multiple cycles – real wealth is going to be built by stringing together multiple full market cycles.

I can almost guarantee that at some time in your investing career, you will feel *'The market really should have gone up by now.'* It will not be fun at that stage, and that's OK.

If we remove all emotion from it, if we have our strategy and we stick to it, if we can be patient and play the long game while continuing to learn and evolve, it's not a question of if you will win; it's when you will win and to what size.

3. Own the Outcomes

From being a coach and investor for a long time, I've seen that human nature is very predictable. For many investors, if everything is going great, they are high-fiving, and everyone is happy.

But as soon as there is a problem, such as a major downturn in the market, it turns into a *'blame game'* instead of *"This is my ship. I'm going to take the ownership/responsibility and calmly see it through to resolve this thing."*

We need to avoid blaming others at all costs. How many super successful people do you know who blame everyone else as soon as something goes wrong? Not many, right?

Great investors are judged and measured in the times of adversity, not the times of peace. If we think about a ship at sea, the crew doesn't want to see the captain all flustered and upset because the storm is coming. They want to see the captain standing on the deck, calmly calling the orders and steering the ship to get everyone home safely. The captain will be remembered for that, not for how they sailed the ship on a calm, smooth, sunny day.

4. ANTs – Controlling the Subconscious Noise

Everyone sometimes gets what we call 'ANTs' in their subconscious brain.

A – Annoying

N – Negative

T – Thoughts

This is the little voice you hear that doesn't always support you. You will never completely stop it, although we can certainly reduce and control it over time. It's just about what you do with it and how you manage them to minimize its power.

So, this is one technique that I've used over the years…

When I get an ANT, I will ask myself, *"Is that thought helping me or hurting me?"* If it's helping me, I'll keep it and take it on. If it's hurting me, I'll think, "*Has it got any value? Has it got any validity?*" And if not, then my mind will push it away into the distance and replace it with the correct empowering thought. We are training our subconscious brain with *"This, not that."*

Everyone should learn NLP (Neurolinguistic Programming) at some stage to discover how to use advanced strategies to control and master the subconscious mind. Most people never learn how to properly control their monkey mind and effectively leave the running of their subconscious brain to a 'it will be fine' approach rather than one of mastery.

You will never hear from anyone else more than your own chatter in your lifetime. That's why it's important to learn to control it so that you are empowering rather than disempowering your actions and results.

5. Be Positive

"Thoughts and language such as 'why me,' 'here we go again,' 'I seem to always get bad breaks,' etc., start to linger and gain momentum unfortunately. None of this stuff helps, and in fact hinders you and leads to more discouraging thoughts and self-talk! That is because what you put out, is what you get back!" – John Novak, Australian sports motivator and mindset specialist

I think of positivity and negativity as like a world energy magnet. Whichever energy you put into the world is what you will likely attract back into your world.

When you see the world from a negative perspective, you are constantly drawn into a cycle of negative actions and emotions.

When you have a more positive outlook on life, you are far more likely to attract good things to come your way.

Positivity is primarily about having an optimistic outlook and focusing on the good aspects of situations, even when faced with challenges or setbacks. Positive individuals tend to emphasize possibilities and solutions rather than problems and obstacles. They believe that things will work out for the best.

An example of this as it relates to your investing is when there is a market pullback. You can focus on the paper gains you have lost or look at it as another opportunity to deploy more capital before the next rise in the market. I know which one is likely to make you more successful over time.

The subconscious brain deals in exacts, and it gives us what we focus on, so it's super important that we are focused on the positive. This will result in more positives in our lives. We want to avoid replaying negative stories in our minds and, in effect, getting them again and again.

A negative mind will never give you a positive life. It always comes down to mindset. When you think positive, the world around you will become more positive.

Your diet is not only what you eat. It's also who you hang around, what you watch, what you listen to and what you read. I try to live a 100% positive mental diet wherever I can. Obviously, you'll get negative inputs like the news at times, but we should always try to limit those. Is your mental diet helping you or hurting you?

6. *Confidence*

Two tennis players are getting ready to go out on the court. Player one thinks, *"I've got this, I've done the work, I can beat him."* Player two thinks, *"I've seen his serve speed; this isn't going to be good."* If you were a betting man or woman, who would you guess would win? The smart money would be on the more confident person.

So instinctively, you know this, but are you doing it 100% of the time? A wise man once told me, *"To know and not to do is not to really know."*

Being positive and being confident are related but different concepts. As previously discussed, being positive is about your overall outlook on life. Confidence involves a strong belief in your abilities, skills, and judgment. Confident people trust that they can handle various situations effectively.

Being confident can have a massive positive impact on your investing. Being a confident individual means that you are self-assured and less likely to doubt your actions or decisions. The flow-on effect is that you are more willing to take controlled risks because you believe in your ability to succeed.

Self-confidence is like a superpower. Once you start believing in yourself, you hold yourself differently, you communicate differently, you act differently, others treat you differently, and magic starts to happen.

I remember this distinctively when I was a young man. There was a guy who was just an average fellow, 18. There was nothing special about his looks or anything, but he was a bit of a ladies' man. I remember one of my friends asking him, *"How are you doing that? How come all the girls like you?"* And he replied, *"It's simple. The key is confidence."*

I never forgot what he said. Of course, that's just an example of a teenage guy trying to pick up girls. Still, it applies to investing, business, and many other aspects of life.

If you are not confident, you can subconsciously sabotage everything else that is going on. The good news is that as you get a few runs of success on the board, you have more fuel for the fire of your confidence because *'we can do this'* can change to *'we have done this before, and we'll do it again, but even bigger and better this time.'*

7. Abundance Mindset

"Thoughts become things. If you see it in your mind, you will hold it in your hand." – Bob Proctor

In his best-selling book *The Seven Habits of Highly Effective People*, Stephen Covey first described the abundance mindset. Covey defines it as *"a concept in which a person believes there are enough resources and successes to share with others."*

This is the opposite of the scarcity mindset, which is based on the idea that if you win, someone else loses. The origins of this often come from how many people are programmed by older generations as kids with incorrect mindsets such as *'money doesn't grow on trees,' 'money is the root of all evil,'* and the equally inaccurate programming of *'all rich people are bad.'*

To be successful as investors and entrepreneurs, we must live by the belief and knowledge of, *"If I get ahead in life, it doesn't mean that there's not enough for you to get ahead in life as well."*

When it comes down to it, we need to have an abundance mindset to be successful in investing. If we feel that there is not enough money and resources to go around, then this is likely to be a limiting belief that holds us back and sabotages us at a subconscious level.

While there is an element of truth to the fact that not everyone wins with investing, there is nothing that we can do about that because money has always and will always flow from those who don't know what they are doing to those who do know what they are doing.

From a socially conscious point of view, the way I look at this is that I always share knowledge to help others get ahead and increase their chances of winning. I also know that as a poor man, I can do very little, but as a wealthy man, I can have far more leverage and do far more good in the world around me.

8. Resilience

"The world ain't all sunshine and rainbows. It's a very mean and nasty place, and I don't care how tough you are, it will beat you to your knees and keep you there permanently if you let it. You, me, or nobody is gonna hit as hard as life. But it ain't about how hard you hit. It's about how hard you can get hit and keep moving forward; how much you can take and keep moving forward. That's how winning is done!" – Rocky Balboa from the 2006 film *Rocky Balboa*

While that is true in boxing, I have certainly found it true in investing, entrepreneurship, and life.

Resilience has really been the key to a lot my success over the years. Over the years, I have failed at many different business opportunities, investments, and things in life that just didn't pan out the way I wanted.

The real difference between me and most people who started at the same time as me, was that I just kept picking myself up, dusting myself off, figuring out what I could learn from it, and keeping going.

History has shown that sometimes, things that I think went badly actually were a good thing over time because of what I learned from them or how they changed the sequence of events that followed. Often, it's a case of *"Life happened for me, not to me."*

I have often seen people give up just before they were about to strike gold. Don't let this be you. Never give up on your dreams. If you want it bad enough, make it happen.

There is a balancing act here because there are times when a pivot (change in direction) is required so we don't keep smashing our heads into the same brick wall if things are not working.

Often, it's about timing and being ready for the right opportunity at the right time when you are ready to capitalize on it with the right mindset.

Resilience is one of the main differences between people who make it and people who don't.

To quote the great fictional character from the brilliant TV series *Peaky Blinders*, Thomas Shelby, he famously says, *"I have no limitations."* I love this statement because living a limitless life isn't about never encountering limitations. It's about knowing how to respond when challenges arise as you pursue your goals. Remind yourself that can overcome anything that tries to get in your way. Live by this statement, and you'll be amazed at what you can accomplish!

9. Handle Uncertainty

"People will choose unhappiness over uncertainty." – Tim Ferriss, American entrepreneur, investor, author and podcaster

The amazing coach Tony Robbins advises in his teachings that we have two conflicting human needs. One is certainty, and the other is uncertainty (variety).

Certainty is the need for safety, stability, and comfort. It involves the desire to feel secure and to avoid pain or discomfort. People seek certainty to gain a sense of control over their environment and their lives.

Uncertainty, or variety, is the need for change, new stimuli, and adventure. This need is about seeking the unknown and embracing new experiences. It is essential for keeping life exciting and stimulating.

If you look back on a crypto chart, it's very easy to see when you should have bought, held, or sold over time. Unfortunately, we don't have the benefit of hindsight when making an investment.

The reality is that to be successful investors, we must be able to handle uncertainty. We need to do our research, understand where we are in the market cycle based on history or technical analysis, look for the dips as good buying opportunities and then back ourselves to take the plunge and make the investments.

Plenty of times, I've bought different cryptocurrencies thinking they're about to go on a massive upward run, only to find them in a several-month downward spiral. In these cases, I just remove all emotion from it and hold the course, knowing that if I play the long game, I will win in the long run.

10. Get Uncomfortable

"You won't achieve greatness by staying in your comfort zone. Embrace challenges." – Alex Becker

The saying, *"Everything we want is on the other side of our comfort zone,"* has really helped me over time. When I think about my investing and entrepreneurial career, I had to get uncomfortable many times, but looking back, I realise that this is what helped me grow.

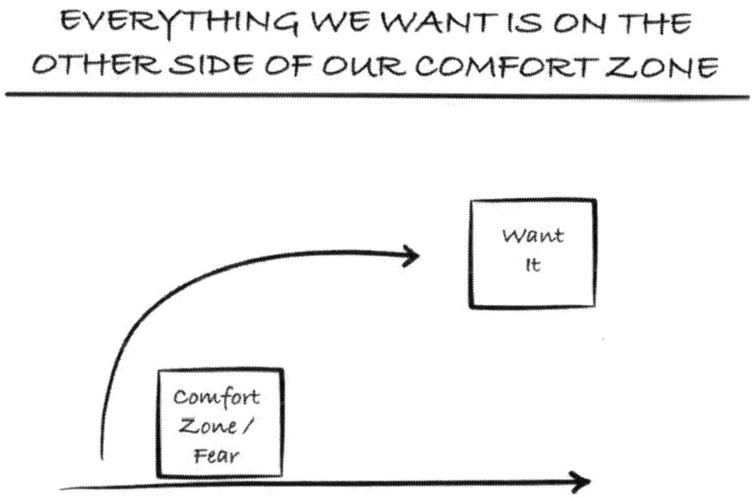

I think of it as layers of improvement. Over time, as we handle more and more difficult problems and can handle higher degrees of stress without letting it affect us, we show up as a higher-valued, more evolved and improved version of ourselves.

I believe that in life, wealth is a scorecard that everyone gets. You get paid in direct proportion to the difficulty of the problems you can solve and the level of stress and pressure that you can confidently handle.

If we don't get uncomfortable by taking some risks and putting our money on the line, what chance do we have of getting on some big 10X – 100X type winners? Not much, right?

It's fair to say we must get uncomfortable to get comfortable. If we want an easy life in the future, we may have to have a bit of a hard life now. If we have an easy life now, we're likely to have a hard life in the future, so it's best to get uncomfortable now.

11. Speed

A saying that I live by is, *'Success follows speed.'* I have found this to be true in business, investing and life.

Have you ever been to a restaurant with a friend, and it takes them 20 minutes to decide what to order? I know people who find it takes them longer to decide what they are going to order than it takes for the chef to cook their food. But how successful are these people?

Go to dinner with a bunch of multi-millionaires, and they will scan the menu and quickly decide because it's a non-core decision. As long as it's relatively healthy, it doesn't make much difference.

I like this about the power of speed from the entrepreneur and business mentor, Alex Hormozi. To quote Alex, *"You can move through life at 7 times the rate of other people by simply changing when you say you are going to make a decision from end of week to end of day. How is that guy so young and he's achieved so much? Well, what takes you a month to make a decision, we make in an hour, and then in the next hour I make another decision that takes you your next month. That is how you can go 30 times faster than the average person who's overweight, has $1,000 in their bank account and is going to die at 70."*

This applies to investing. You do your research, you have your dry powder. If your gut feel is good and the marketing timing feels right, then just go for it and pull the trigger with your investment. Will the buy price be better in two weeks' time? Maybe, but inversely, it may also be a lot more expensive. Success follows speed, so make quick decisions and back yourself.

12. Learn Not Fail

"An investment in knowledge pays the best interest." – Benjamin Franklin.

School is such a formative part of our lives. We really learned a lot there, but the reality is that they teach things to set you up to work hard for the rest of your life, not how to work smart and really get ahead.

At school, you do tests, and everything is focused on *'you must pass'* and *'do not fail.'* The most successful people in entrepreneurship, investing and life change that mindset and do not worry about failing. The reality is they failed at lots of things, they sucked at lots of things, and that's just fine.

Life is about learning from failures and iterating. Effectively, it's flicking a switch in your mindset when things go wrong from the natural thought pattern of *"I'll never do that again"* to the more empowering thought pattern of *"What lessons can we take from that?"*

Warren Buffett famously said, *"The first rule of an investment is don't lose money. And the second rule of an investment is don't forget the first rule."* So, obviously, when investing, we need to try to preserve our capital and not lose it. But there will be times when market timing doesn't go your way or when an investment decision doesn't pan out the way you thought it would.

We want to minimize the downside, but the good thing about investing if we are playing the multi-cycle game is that we take the lessons from any setbacks, remove any emotion from them, and step up to the plate again when the timing is right. The great thing is that with investing, you always get another swing at the bat, and if you keep swinging, at some point, you are going to smash one out of the park.

Chapter 13 – Essential Financial IQ For Building Wealth

Most People Retire Broke

At school, you are not taught how to handle money, the rules of money or anything about financial IQ. This is a major reason I believe self-education is more important than the formal education you have received through the system.

Based on the Federal Reserve's Survey of Consumer Finances, data from the Employee Benefit Research Institute revealed that a mere 0.1% of retirees accumulate over $5 million in their retirement accounts, whereas only 3.2% amass over $1 million.

This means that most people in the US and the broader world are retiring with not much of a nest egg, given the growing cost of living from inflation.

The good thing is you are in the right spot at the right time. You are learning about investing in the fastest-growing investment asset class of all time, and hopefully, following this, you will take massive action to stand out from the masses.

Be Careful Where You Get Your Advice

"If you're not in the arena also getting your ass kicked, I'm not interested in your feedback." – Brené Brown, American professor, social worker, author and podcaster

Throughout my life, especially when I was younger, I have had many people advise me about money, investing and business. While all of them meant well, when I think about it, many of these people retired broke or close to it.

Brené has nailed it with that one statement above. If the person giving you advice has no experience in the area or a similar area, then take it on board but *'with a grain of salt.'*

Instead, seek out mentors and coaches who have already achieved what you are working towards. I think this applies to our investing, too. If the person giving you advice doesn't have a sizable portfolio and a large track record of success, I'd give it less weight than what you are learning here with this book and the companion training series.

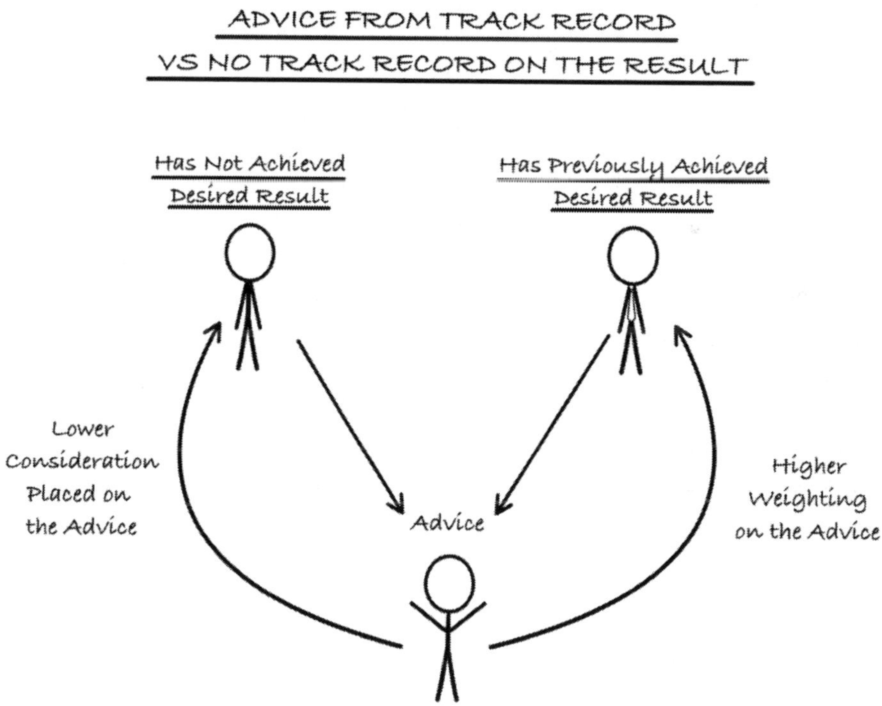

Ultimately, in life, we want high income with low stress.

I learned about the concept of *Coolness Factor'* from the American marketing strategist and consultant, Carl White. I saw him teach it on stage and it impacted me straight away. I never forgot it because it gave me a great framework for looking at businesses and investing to see if they met my gut feeling of being worthy of my time.

If we want to build a business and investment portfolio with a high coolness factor, it needs to be high income and low stress.

COOLNESS FACTOR IN YOUR INVESTING, BUSINESS & LIFE

$$\text{Coolness Factor} = \frac{\text{Income}}{\text{Stress}}$$

$$\text{Income} \downarrow \; = \; \downarrow \text{Coolness}$$

$$\text{Stress} \uparrow \; = \; \downarrow \text{Coolness}$$

If our income goes down, our coolness goes down. And if our stress goes up, our coolness goes down. So that's why, at times, I've had to change investment vehicles, sack clients, move on from business partners or sack team members because, whether they knew it or not, their coolness factor wasn't working for me. Even though there was money in it, it just wasn't worth the time or stress.

For me, the coolness factor is an amazing concept to live by. How is the coolness factor in your business and investing? What could you do to reduce your stress and/or raise your income while at the same time making you happier?

Learn the Rules to the Game of Money

The harsh reality in life is that either you are going to master money, or you are going to be a slave to it your whole life.

As a child, I was always told to *'work hard.'* While this is valid, I believe a better approach is to *'work smart.'*

We can't just work hard and hope to become wealthy. We need to have a different plan so that we don't do the same thing as everyone else and expect a different result.

Financial freedom comes from getting more leverage in our lives (by getting our money working for us) and learning the rules of the game of money.

Imagine if you didn't know the rules of football; what are your chances of winning? Not high. You're going to keep getting penalized and have setback after setback, while your opposition, who knows the rules of the game, is going to be able to capitalize on your mistakes. The same thing applies to the game of money.

10 Financial IQ Wealth Creation Lessons

Your wealth creation and financial security are more important than any game of football, so let's invest some time together in learning the rules of the game. Here are 10 financial IQ wealth creation lessons to help you to be more successful on your investing journey.

1. *Get Your Money Working For You Rather Than You Working for Money*

For a large part of my career, I worked jobs and built businesses to build wealth. While this did work, it was a plan that had its limitations because of the lack of leverage. Later in life, I learned that *'he or she who gets the most leverage wins.'*

If you look at nearly every billionaire in the world, what do they do? They build businesses and use that money to invest. I was doing the first half but missed out on the second half.

I now use business to fund my lifestyle and investing, which is how I have built most of my wealth.

You need to get money working for you rather than you working for money. I first learned this when I read Robert Kiyosaki's *Rich Dad, Poor Dad.* If you haven't read that or the *Cashflow Quadrant* book that follows it, I strongly recommend you do, as they really changed my life profoundly.

You might have a day job or a business, but by investing using our five-part 'Crypto Pentagon' plan, you are now getting your money working for you rather than you just working for money.

As you get good at it, you'll notice that at times, like during a bull run, your money will start making far more money than you do, which is very exciting indeed.

The British entrepreneur Steven Bartlett has an amazing saying about this: *"Make your money be like soldiers, where every day it goes out, takes prisoners and comes back with more."*

2. *Build Both Cash Flow and Net Worth*

I've had times in my life when I've had good cash flow but no investments to grow my net worth. I've also had times where I've had good investments but not enough cash flow to cover the running of my household, paying my bills and getting ahead.

The reality is that we need both. Ideally, we need a business or income stream that provided us with dry powder cash so that we can feed the beast (put more funds into our investments) and produce cash for us to live off and fund our lifestyle.

We need cash flow so we don't need to kill or hurt the golden goose to survive and thrive. We will go deeper into this golden goose concept later in this chapter.

NEED BOTH CASH FLOW & NET WORTH

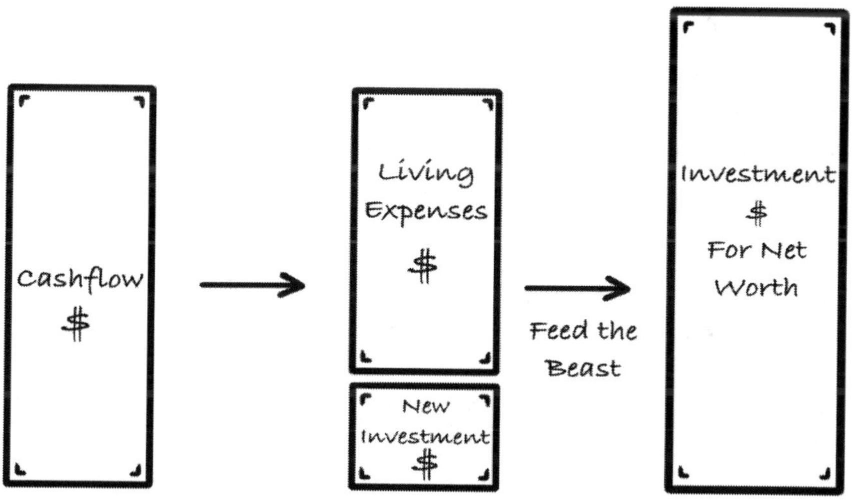

3. Pay Yourself First Like the Rich

"Do not save what is left after spending but spend what is left after saving." – Warren Buffett

The rich pay themselves first with money (to have money to invest), then pay their bills and everything else.

The poor and middle class spend first and only save or invest what is left at the end of the month (which is often not much or anything at all).

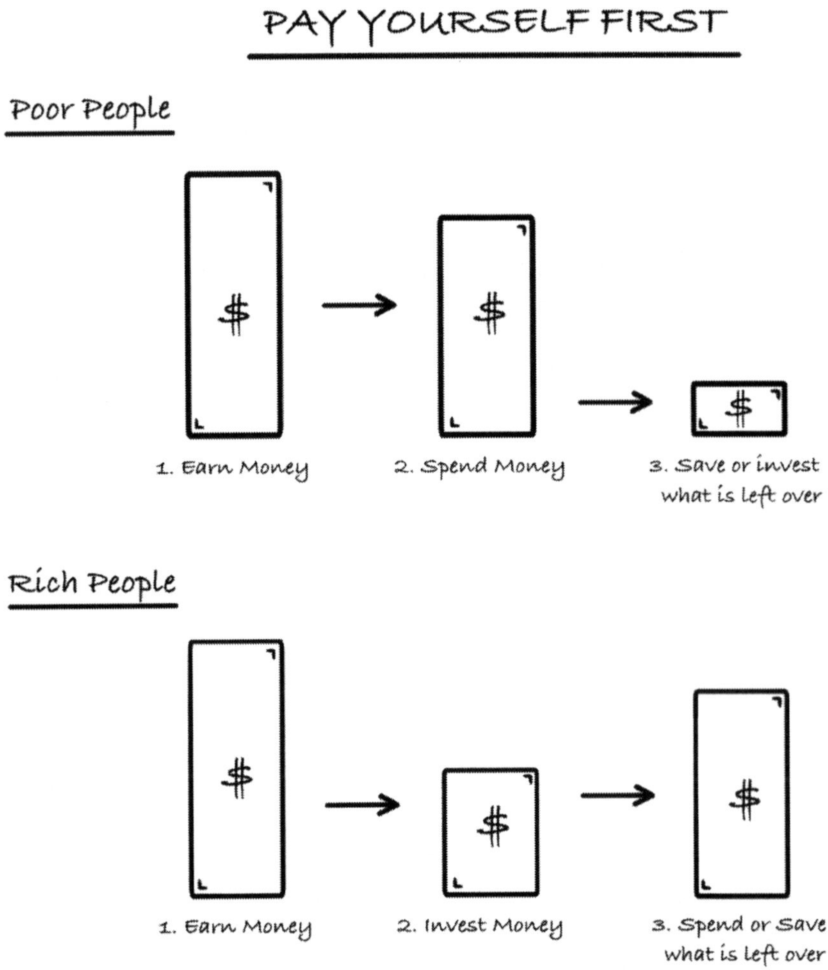

This one little thing of paying yourself first for investing (even if it's only 5% or 10% of your income) and then only spending what is left is a very hard discipline to master initially, but it will make a massive difference over time. If you can automate it, do it.

Rich people also always pay themselves first with their time. At the start of the day, I will work on my knowledge, investing and growing my businesses before I even look at emails or do meetings. I find it best to leave the mornings free for productive work that moves you forward and do meetings and actions for other people, such as in emails, later in the day. This way, we pay ourselves first with time, like the rich.

4. *Create Additional Income – Learn and Action Specialized Skills*

A common problem I see is when people's expenses nearly match their income or, in many cases, exceed their income, so they are going backward. I've been guilty of that a few times, especially when I was just starting in the workforce.

The problem with this approach is that it leaves very little in the way of funds for investing, and it's stressful as you are going backward or not going forward at all financially.

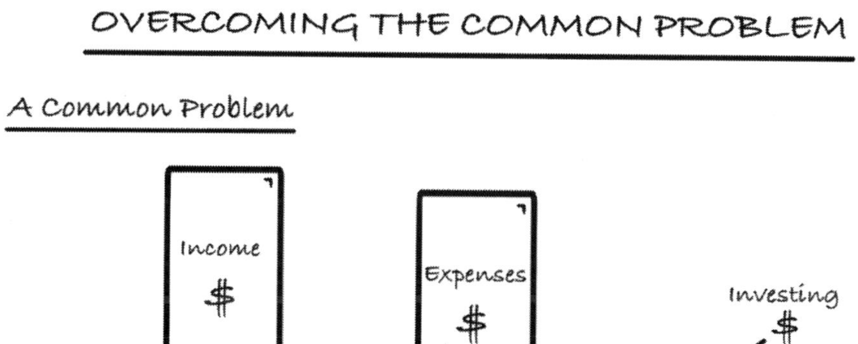

In that scenario we need more spare cash for investment income. There are only two main ways of doing it: creating new additional income or reducing our expenses.

A combination of these two strategies can really free up cash and give you more dry powder cash ready for investing.

Thomas C. Corley reported on CNBC that he did a five-year study of 233 wealthy people for his book *Rich Habits*. From that he found:

- 65 percent had three streams of income
- 45 percent had four streams of income
- 29 percent had five or more streams of income

One is the worst number in business. Most people have one income stream: their *'good, safe job.'* But this is also risky because you put all your eggs in one basket, and that boss can very easily tell you, *"Thanks, but we don't need you anymore"* (and you have lost all your income in one move).

Additional income streams could come from improving your existing job or business, or additional businesses or side hustles.

There's a concept called specialized skills. If you are in a job, the fastest way often to get a pay rise is to significantly increase your specialized skills. A good way to do this is to study and get certified by an industry body in whatever you do. As you become more senior at what you do, you will likely keep getting paid more and more. That's going to allow you to invest on a bigger level.

If you don't have the spare capital right now to get certified by an industry body, we also have this other incredible technology at our fingertips called the Internet. Instead of spending that 30–60 minutes a night watching Netflix, spend that time improving your specialized skills on the Internet. You are only limited by your imagination of what you can learn online, often for free or at a very low cost.

Even with your specialized skill, though, it's still limited to one income stream. Another option is to build a side hustle or a business. With the Gig Economy now, it's very easy to get additional income with a side hustle using services such as Uber, Fiver, Upwork or a range of other gig economy services.

The other main option is to build a side business. Common online ones include affiliate marketing, eCommerce, selling courses, becoming an influencer and drop shipping.

Give it some thought – how could you build another income stream or two? Once again, the Internet and YouTube, in particular, is a great place to start thinking of these ideas.

5. Reduce Expenses for More Profit to Allocate to Your Investing

In the section above, we looked at the common problem of expenses exceeding income, or having little spare cash left over for investing.

We covered the first main answer to this problem: *'Create additional income streams.'* The second answer is we need to *'reduce our expenses.'*

'Live below your means' is a financial principle that encourages individuals to spend less money than they earn. It's widely known but not always well adopted.

Most people seem to spend everything they earn, or worse, more than they earn. A lesson I needed to learn the hard way over time was, *"It's not how much money you make. It's how much money you keep."*

I was guilty of this when I had a job in my younger years. I can still remember that for several pay rises, my wife and I had already planned how we would spend the money before it had even hit our bank account.

Over time, we learned to change our mindset from *'spend'* to *'invest.'*

Reducing costs is a very impactful strategy to get spare investing money.

If we increase our income by a thousand dollars a month, that's not necessarily direct profit. The reason is that often, there are costs of producing that income or taxes that we must pay on it. But if we reduce our costs by a thousand dollars a month, that's direct profit. So that will give us more money to accelerate our investing.

How long has it been since you have reviewed your bank or credit card statements? Are there any costs you can cut out to reduce your expenses?

6. Start Investing Early & Often

"Compound interest is the eighth wonder of the world. He who understands it, earns it. He who doesn't, pays it." – Albert Einstein

In Chapter 8, we explored the power of multiple cycles and showed that the professional investor plays the longer multi-cycle game, which allows us to multiply the tokens and the gains.

Imagine if you started stringing together bull and bear cycles one or two times before your actual start date – would you be significantly ahead now? Chances are the answer is a confident *'Yes,'* especially with what you have been learning with this book and the accompanying video training.

Starting investing earlier in life and investing when you have spare dry powder at good times in the market cycle offers many significant benefits for you including:

- *Compound interest:* One of the most significant advantages of starting early is the power of compound interest. The earlier you start investing, the more time your investments have to grow exponentially. Compounding can turn small, regular investments into substantial sums over time.

- *Time horizon:* With a longer investment horizon, you can ride out market fluctuations and have a higher potential for growth. Time allows for recovery from market downturns and benefits from the overall upward trend of markets.
- *Lower risk:* Investing early allows for a more aggressive investment strategy, potentially yielding higher returns. As you get older, you can gradually shift to more conservative investments to protect your accumulated wealth.
- *Financial discipline:* Regular investing fosters good financial habits. It encourages saving, budgeting, and making informed financial decisions, contributing to overall financial health.
- *Achieving financial goals:* Starting early gives you a better chance of achieving long-term financial goals, such as buying a home, funding education, or retiring comfortably. The sooner you start, the more achievable these goals become without needing to invest large sums later in life.

Overall, the combination of time, compounding, and disciplined investing can significantly enhance one's financial well-being and help one achieve one's long-term financial aspirations.

7. Build Cash Reserves for Buying the Dip Opportunities and Rainy Days

CNBC recently reported that 78% of Americans are living paycheck to paycheck. I understand this when we start out in the workforce and in business, but over time, we need to use the *'pay yourself first'* approach to build some cash reserve in a bank account that we don't touch.

This gives you certainty with some money to fall back on to *'weather the storm'* if something bad happens, like a downturn in your business or losing your job.

Part of freedom is the freedom of choice of who you work with and when. Cash reserves give you choices because you don't have to make decisions like *'we better work with them even though they are not a good person because we need the money.'* This has a flow-on effect on your energy and state of mind.

Several times throughout my investing career, I have seen amazing new opportunities or buying opportunities following market corrections. Multiple times, I have missed these moments because I didn't have cash reserves or dry powder ready to deploy when I needed it.

I've now learned from that mistake and try to always have some cash reserves to weather a storm or capitalize on opportunities.

8. Develop / Earn Your Dual Black Belt to Win the Game

I've figured out the 'Dual Black Belt' strategy in recent years, and it's helped lots of people see the bigger picture and engineer a brighter financial future. I hope you *'get it'* and that it impacts you, too.

Earlier in this chapter, we discussed that we need both cash flow and net worth. Ideally, a business or income stream provides us with dry powder cash so that we can feed the beast (put more funds into our investments) while producing cash for us to live off and fund our lifestyle.

In martial arts, the well-known concept of earning your black belt through knowledge, hard work, and discipline is a sign that you really know your stuff and are an expert at your craft.

I meet many entrepreneurs who laser-focus on learning marketing, sales, and business. Effectively, they earn their conceptual black belt there, but they miss the leverage and compounding of investing.

You want to develop and earn your dual black belt to win the game. Dual black belt means we become great at marketing, sales and business and then also master investing.

If you can get really good at business and investing, this is like a one plus one equals three. Most people don't even focus on mastery of one of those. If you can get both black belts, this incredible strategy will set you up for life.

9. Keep Rather Than Spend the Golden Goose

Let's define our golden goose as *'our total investment profits at our disposal at the end of the bull market.'*

"I'm not working anymore; I'm going full time into crypto investing," my friend John proudly advised after he had been learning from me and implementing the exact same stuff that you learned in part 1 of this book.

"How are you going to fund your lifestyle and living expenses?" I asked. The reply was, *"I'll just sell some of my investments."*

While it does work once you have a large enough portfolio, it's not normally recommended in your first cycle or two because of the flow-on effect of spending your golden goose (your investment profits).

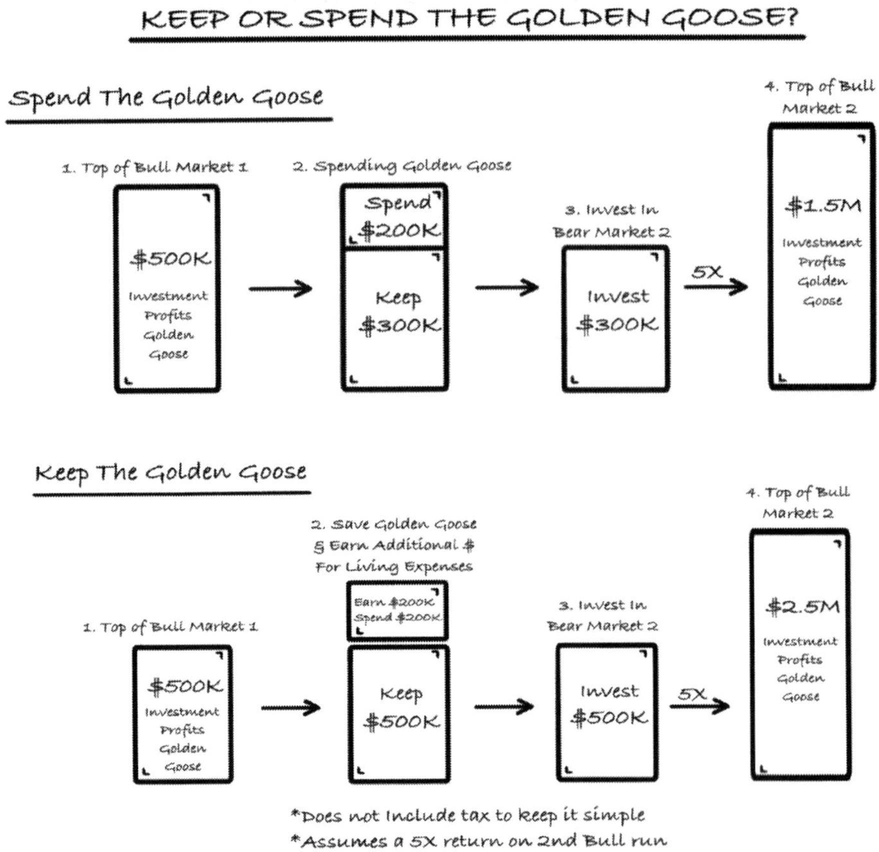

In the example above, you can see that by spending $200K from the golden goose it had an opportunity cost of $1M over the four-year cycle, because the amount invested into the next cycle was only $300K instead of $500K. When multiplied with a 5x return over the cycle that followed, it resulted in a $1.5M investment golden goose instead of a possible $2.5M golden goose.

"But $1.5M is still lots of money, Troy, it doesn't really matter," you may be thinking.

How about if we add another cycle onto that and do the same thing again? How does it look now?

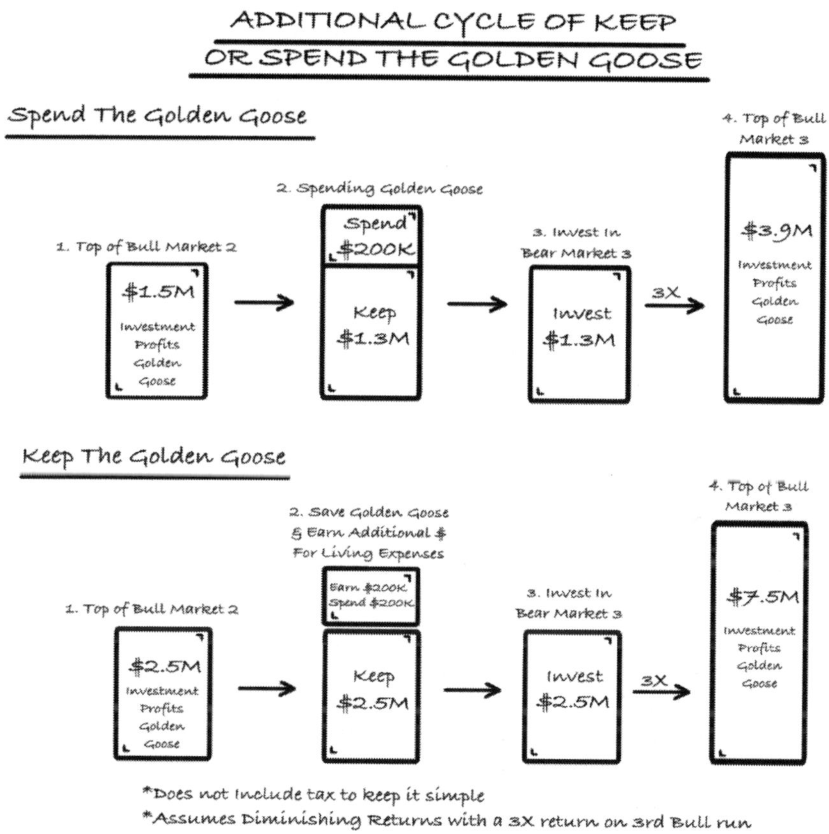

You can see the flow-on effect of spending $400K out of the golden goose over two cycles: a massive $3.6M in potential golden goose investment profits.

But I acknowledge that we only live once and never know what is around the corner, so life is there for the living. My late, amazing friend Kevin Mendoza lived every day like it was his last and had an incredible life. He was taken far too young, but he ensured that his legacy lives on. You need to get that fine balance between the two – investing for the future and living every day like it's your last.

I am taking profits off the table between cycles to buy fun things like family trips and a family home, but I'm not just starting on my journey.

When it comes down to it, I think there really is no right or wrong answer. It's about what works best for you when balancing money and lifestyle now vs. future money and lifestyle.

10. Watch & Manage Your Own 401K / Superannuation Investments

A 401(k) is defined as *"a tax-advantaged retirement savings plan offered by many U.S. employers, allowing employees to contribute a portion of their salary to individual accounts, often with employer matching contributions, which can grow tax-deferred until withdrawal."*

In other parts of the world, it has different names. In Australia, it is called Superannuation; the Canadians call it a Registered Retirement Savings Plan (RRSP) and the British call it a Personal Pension or Workplace pension. Depending on where you live, yours may have a different name, but I think you get the concept.

No one cares about your financial security as much as you do. But what is weird is that most people *'outsource their long-term wealth management.'* They don't choose to get their investing black belt and manage it themselves.

In Australia, you can manage your own superannuation fund, which is called a Self-Managed Superannuation Fund (SMSF). Other countries use different terms for the same financial structure concept, often using the words Self-Directed, Self-Managed, Self-Administrated or Self-Invested.

Win the game with multiple structures. Many of the things we've been talking about so far have been with your own personal money, but what about if you now switch to a self-managed retirement fund and apply the same investing you have been learning here? It's probably not a good move when you are first getting started. Still, over time, as you master your craft, it could really bear fruit and dramatically change your retirement funds.

MULTIPLE 4 YEAR CYCLES

WITH PERSONAL & 401K/SUPERANNUATION MONEY

Personal Money

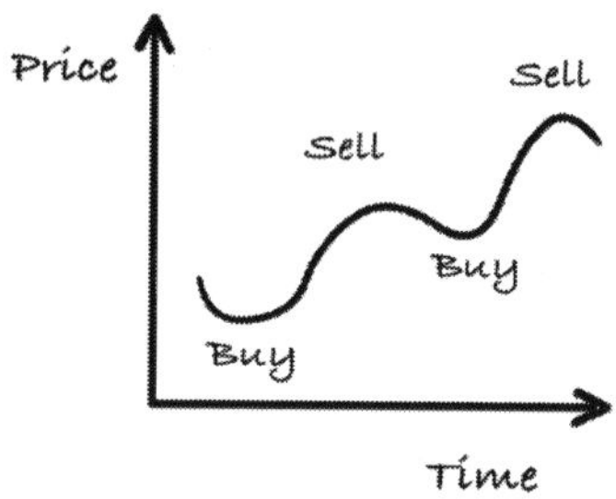

401K Money

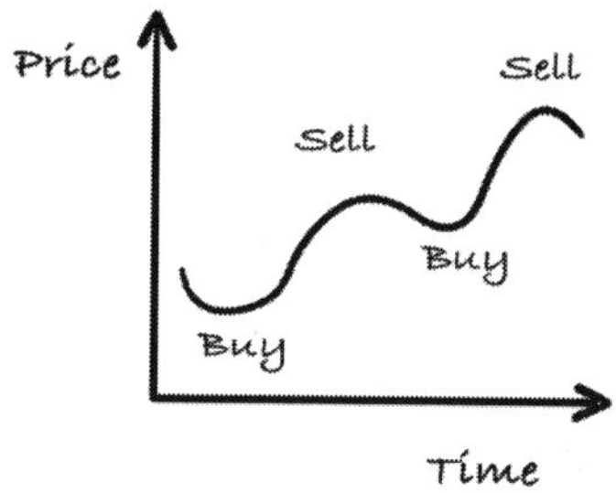

Chapter 14 – Your Dream Life By Design

"The only true test of intelligence is if you get what you wanted out of life." – Naval Ravikant

The Greatest Wealth Creation Opportunity of Our Lifetime

Most people just leave life to chance. They hope and pray that everything will work out fine and that they will get everything they ever wanted. We don't want to do that.

Naval's statement above is very wise. It effectively says that if you get what you want out of life, you're smart. If you don't, you're not. But an even more important question is embedded in the premise of the first: Are you wise enough to know what you want to begin with?

We need to be crystal clear about exactly what we want from our lives and then engineer it to make it happen.

As we covered in Chapter 1, this is the greatest wealth-creation opportunity of our lifetimes.

Crypto is the best investment opportunity ever given to retail investors like you and me. This is also the first time in history that retail investors have been able to front run (get into a market) and obtain better buy prices than institutional investors.

It's the best-performing asset class of all time, the fastest-adopted technology outside of AI, and the fastest-generating wealth in the shortest period of time.

The prize of getting this right is freedom and your dream life by design. The prize is also the security of knowing that you've got some good rainy-day funds locked away and parked in property or whatever vehicle you chose so that you are in a strong position regarding life and stress reduction.

Life is a series of moments. If your life was a movie, what scenes would you put into your feature film to make it awesome?

We Can't Do the Same as Everyone Else and Expect a Different Result

"If you think trying is risky, wait till you get the bill for not trying." – Jim Rohn

I have found that we all want these four things.

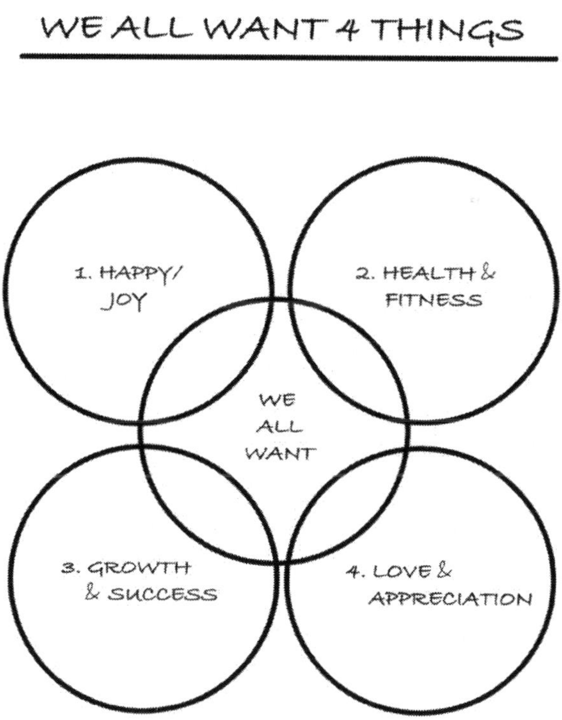

Most people achieve some of these. With some work and engineering the results, I believe it's all 100% achievable to get all four of these for both you and me. The question then becomes not '*if you can do it?*' but '*will you do it*?'

We can't do the same thing as everyone else and expect a different result. We must be willing to do what others won't do to get results that others want but will never achieve. Let's now look at a simplified version of our high-level plan to get you on the fast track to wealth creation and make designing your dream life much easier.

Hardware & Operating System

Let's break some of the key learnings we have covered into layers that build on each other. The first is the Hardware and Operating System.

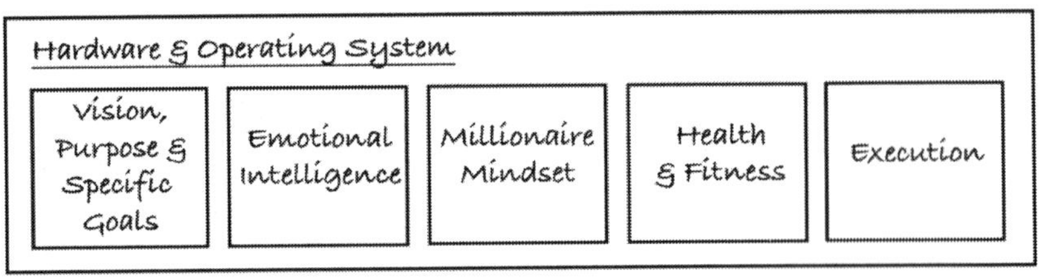

"You bring yourself to the deal." This is about showing up as the very best version of yourself with your investing. This is working on the '*who do I need to become?*' to achieve the next level of success.

Do you know what you want out of life? Do you have a clear vision of what it is you are building? Have you broken that down into meaningful specific goals so that your subconscious brain can go to work on those?

Our mindset and emotions are as much as 80% of our success. This is perhaps the most important area to continue learning and improving in, as it will either assist you in getting where you want to go or hold you back if you have blockages or issues there.

We need to be healthy and fit, plus take massive action as success follows speed.

Financial IQ & Specialized Skills

This is essential financial knowledge for turbocharging our investing.

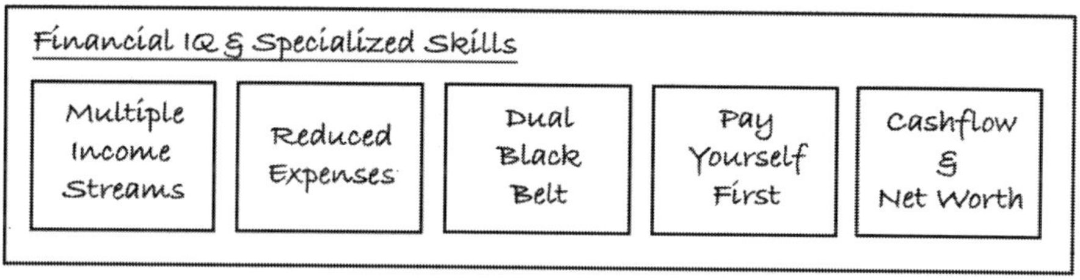

We need to build both cash flow and net worth. Things like paying ourselves first, reducing our expenses and creating multiple streams of income are crucial for having more dry powder to be able to invest more.

The Dual Black Belt in both business and investing is a proven winner, so that you will never struggle with cash flow or investment gains again. We will use business to fund our expenses, lifestyle and investing, and use investing to build wealth over time.

Investing Advantage

Most investors get wrecked and don't make significant gains. This is largely because they don't invest enough into their knowledge and don't know and play by the rules of the game.

Investing is a marathon, not a sprint. We give ourselves an advantage by playing a long-term game over multiple cycles. By starting early, continually investing at opportune times, and re-investing a portion of the gains from last cycle, we transition from *'will I win?'* to *'I am going to win over the longer term.'*

Investing Strategy

At school, we are not taught this stuff. Throughout my years of formal education, no one ever mentioned, *"Here is how to get your money to grow so you don't have to work hard all your lif*e."

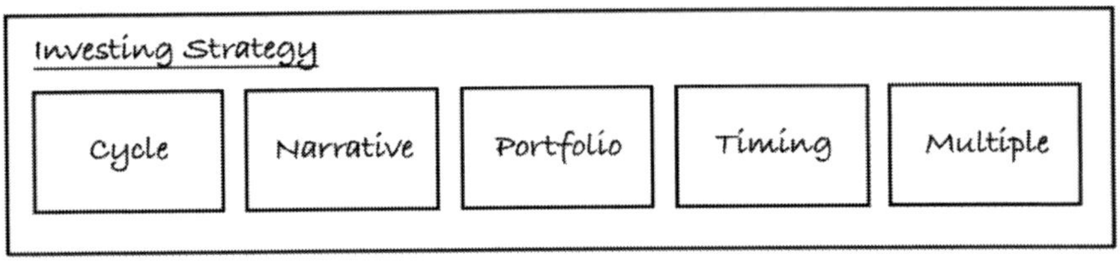

This Crypto Pentagon strategy is crucial for crypto investors' long-term success. If you don't understand the four-year cycle, you will hand your money over to those who do.

We need to identify trending narratives with money flowing into them and use that information to make project purchase decisions when designing and structuring high-growth portfolios that also reduce our risk of failure.

By playing the long game over multiple cycles and timing correctly when to get in and out, we can outperform most investors and create life-changing wealth.

Dream Life By Design

Most people leave life to chance, hoping and praying that it will all work out just fine. I find this approach flawed and believe it can lead to stress and an average life rather than an extraordinary one.

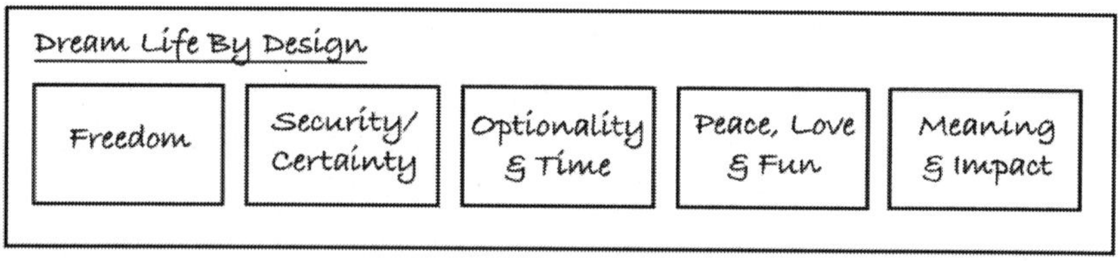

I engineer everything to happen so that I have excellent cash flow and nest egg wealth, which allows me to have the freedom to live where I want, travel where I want, and choose when I do and don't want to work.

Building a large portfolio has given me security and certainty in my life. This means I don't have to worry about money, and I can weather any storm if something bad happens. I want the exact same for you coming up if you are not there already.

Over the years, I traded time for money. Now that I have money, I'm using it to buy back the most precious resource that we can't ever get back: time. Optionality means that I have positioned my skills, brand, authority and wealth to the point where I'm not forced to do things that I don't want to do. I have good options.

I'm a big believer in *'engineering more fun'* and building an amazing life CV, while hanging out with people I love. As a poor man, the amount of good I could do in the world was limited. With wealth creation, I can now engineer a more positive impact in the world around me, to hopefully leave the world a little better than how I found it.

Putting It All Together

Below is the logical model for the whole Crypto New Rich system. Check it out and identify areas you are doing well in and also areas that you now know you need to focus on.

THE CRYPTO NEW RICH

Bring The Best Version of You to Your Investing, Business & Life For the Prize of Freedom & Your Dream Life by Design

Dream Life By Design

Freedom	Security/ Certainty	Optionality & Time	Peace, Love & Fun	Meaning & Impact

Investing Strategy

Cycle	Narrative	Portfolio	Timing	Multiple

Investing Advantage

Invest Early & Often	Feed the Beast	Reinvest Golden Goose	The Long Game	Continual Research & Learning

Financial IQ & Specialized Skills

Multiple Income Streams	Reduced Expenses	Dual Black Belt	Pay Yourself First	Cashflow & Net Worth

Hardware & Operating System

Vision, Purpose & Specific Goals	Emotional Intelligence	Millionaire Mindset	Health & Fitness	Execution

Final Thoughts

The reality is we only have limited time on this earth. The years fly by quickly. So, we may as well figure out exactly what we want out of life and engineer that to happen.

But there is a catch – to get freedom and your dream life by design, you'll need to learn some new stuff, evolve, take massive action and get a bit uncomfortable along the way. But it's all worth it.

The great news is that you and I live in an incredible time in history. The introduction of the *'Internet of money and trust'* is happening only once, and we get to benefit from the fastest-growing asset class of all time.

More good news is that building wealth with crypto is a learnable skill. It's formulaic and repeatable, especially if you work hard on your mindset and emotional intelligence along the way. From reading this book and watching the companion video training, you will now have a better investing knowledge than over 90% of other investors. You know the essentials; now it's just about going out and implementing them.

We live in amazing times; you really can have it all. Think bigger thoughts, dream bigger dreams. Do whatever it takes for as long as it takes to build your freedom and design your dream life.

Work smart, play hard and enjoy the journey.

About the Author

Troy Harris is a digital entrepreneur who discovered the power of blockchain technology in 2016. This led him to invest in cryptocurrencies such as Bitcoin and Ethereum when most people had never heard of them. Some of these cryptocurrency investments have made him gains of well over 5,000%, and his business now owns a multi-million dollar crypto portfolio.

Troy's passion is researching and sharing the latest and most effective strategies for extracting gains from the cryptocurrency market. His success story has led him to speak worldwide and share the stage with world-renowned authors, investors, and economists such as Robert Kiyosaki, Harry Dent, Dr. Deepak Chopra and Peter Schiff.

NEXT STEPS

Download the Free Resources

If you like any of our hand-drawn logical model diagrams and would like to use them to explain complex concepts simply to your audience, please feel free to use and republish them based on the condition that they have our CryptoNewRich.com URL on them.

DOWNLOAD THE FREE RESOURCES

Includes ✓ All the Diagrams from the Book

See CryptoNewRich.com/resources

* We give you full permission to use these visual diagrams in your social posts & communication materials provided they have our branding watermarks as per these free resources.

Crypto New Rich Video Training

Take the time to stop and sharpen your saw with this cost-effective video training. You'll get your desired results faster, while also reducing your risks of making costly mistakes.

**The above-listed investment in your education is risk-free, as we offer a 100% money-back guarantee. In the unlikely event that you have watched the training and did not get amazing value from it, just reach out to our team, and we will refund your money in full.*

Pay It Forward

My team and I believe this book and training will help many people and have a positive impact on many lives.

If you got good value from this, please share CryptoNewRich.com or the link to the Amazon book with your friends who are on a crypto investing journey. They will thank you for it, as it can fast-track their journey to freedom and help them avoid making big mistakes along the way.

Please also give us a review on Amazon as it will help get the word out to others. Thanks.

Printed in Great Britain
by Amazon

59792479R00093